NOVICE

3
Simple Truths
and

6
Essential Traits
of

Powerful Writing

PRESTWICK HOUSE, INC.
"Everything for the English Classroom!"

Simple Truths
and

Essential Traits
of

Powerful Writing

SENIOR EDITOR: Douglas E. Grudzina

EDITOR: Mary C. Beardsley

BOOK DESIGN: Larry Knox

PRODUCTION: Jerry Clark

PRESTWICK HOUSE, INC.

P.O. BOX 658 • CLAYTON, DELAWARE 19938

TEL: 1.800.932.4593

FAX: 1.888.718.9333

WEB: www.prestwickhouse.com

ISBN 978-1-58049-320-8

Table of Contents

Continued on next page

Applying *the* Third Truth

Powerful writing is painless to read.

Simple Truths
and

Essential Traits
of

Powerful Writing

PRESTWICK HOUSE, INC.
"Everything for the English Classroom!"

Essential Traits

OVER THE PAST SEVERAL YEARS, two trends in writing instruction have grown in popularity: primary trait instruction and trait-based scoring. Both of these trends carry great benefits for the students, but their effectiveness is limited by how they are understood and implemented in today's classrooms. The Prestwick House *Simple Truths* series hopes to overcome a few of these limitations.

Primary Trait Instruction comes packaged under a number of names, and is probably the most popular method of teaching writing. It is based on the premise that there are six (some editors opt for five traits, while others promote seven traits; we feel six cover writing instruction best) essential characteristics or "traits" to a piece of writing and that each of these traits can be taught separately. These traits can then be combined at some point to produce a good essay.

Throughout the *Simple Truths* series, we will focus on the traits of **Development and Elaboration, Organization, Sentence Structure and Variety, Conventions of Written English, Word Choice,** and **Voice**. Each of these is explained in its own chapter.

Underlying the Six Essential Traits, however, are three simple principles, or truths, that *explain the need* for each of the traits in powerful writing.

1st Truth — Powerful writing really says something.

ESSENTIAL TRAIT:

❶ Development and Elaboration: Generalizations and ideas are central to powerful writing and they must be well developed.

2nd Truth — Powerful writing is understandable to others.

ESSENTIAL TRAITS:

❷ Organization: Ideas and supporting details must be presented clearly, coherently, and concisely.

❸ Sentence Structure and Variety: Sentences are structured for maximum effect and are marked by variety and clarity.

❹ Conventions of Written English: The conventions of English (punctuation, capitalization, margins) exist to make it easier for the reader to understand the writer's point. When conventions are ignored, readers lose patience trying to follow the writer's thoughts.

3rd Truth — Powerful writing is painless to read.

ESSENTIAL TRAITS:

❺ Word Choice: Words are chosen carefully in order to perform special functions; clichés, trite expressions, and ambiguities are avoided.

❻ Voice: Voice characterizes the speaker behind the words. Voice conveys a message subtly, but powerfully.

Applying
the
First Truth

Powerful writing really says something.

3
Simple Truths
and
6
Essential Traits
of

Powerful Writing

DEVELOPMENT AND ELABORATION

Trait One

TRAIT ONE:
DEVELOPMENT AND ELABORATION

POWERFUL ESSAYS are not just mass collections of words and sentences. They have a point. Although this is most clear in persuasive essays in which the writer clearly wants to "win" an argument, it is also true for informative and personal writing as well. As a writer, think *why* your reader needs to know the information you are sharing. Being clear about the point of your essay will make it much easier for you to decide what information you need to present.

Powerful essays offer the reader information or insight he or she didn't know before. In order for the reader to appreciate your point *fully*, you want to make certain you provide enough details, explanations, definitions, and so on. By the same token, you don't want to clutter your essay—and your reader's mind—with trivial and irrelevant information that doesn't contribute anything but length to your writing.

Make Yours Better!

Note that the main problem with the following essay is it lacks Development and Elaboration.

The Great Chicago Fire

Not much is known about the cause of the Great Chicago Fire of 1871. However, given the weather conditions that summer and the way the city had been built and managed, the most popular story might indeed be true.

- Too brief. Vague. What is the main point?

Chicago firefighters were used to fighting more than one fire a day. They probably would have been able to control the Great Fire, but human error combined with unpredictable Nature to cause this historic disaster.

- Lacks development, or elaboration. What errors? What about Nature?

Thousands of people fled, but the fire chased them. Later that night several homes were completely destroyed, and still later damage to the pumping station made it impossible to even try to fight the fire. Elsewhere in the city, luxurious new hotels and office buildings were destroyed. Ironically, throughout the summer and fall, newspaper editors had pleaded to improve the city's fire protection in order to avoid exactly this type of disaster. Chicago has always been famous for cutting-edge, hard-hitting newspaper reporting. On Monday, one of the divided branches of the fire reached the city limit. Tuesday morning it began to rain, and the flames finally died out, leaving Chicago a burned-out ruin.

- Do fleeing people and destroyed homes advance the main point?

- This statement about newspapers is irrelevant.

- Using days without dates doesn't clarify the sequence of events.

- No conclusion or clear main idea.

Essay Critique

The introduction mentions human error and Nature as contributing to the fire's severity. There is also mention of the possibility of the "most popular story's" being true regarding the cause of the fire, yet there is no further mention of what this story is. There are no specific facts—not even dates—to explain or illustrate what is only vaguely mentioned.

This essay receives a score of **1** on the:

Development and Elaboration Rubric

5 = The main idea of the essay is clear, but the overall discussion is weakened by inconsistent development and elaboration. Some supporting points tend to be underdeveloped (too few details, examples, anecdotes, supporting facts, etc.). Some minor irrelevancies likewise weaken the essay.

4 = DEVELOPING
The main idea of the essay is suggested. There are supporting details with some elaboration, but supporting points are underdeveloped. Some of the points or development my be tangential or irrelevant to the topic, purpose, and audience.

3 = The main idea of the essay is suggested. There are supporting points without elaboration, or some of the elaboration is irrelevant to the topic, purpose, or audience.

2 = The main idea of the essay is suggested. There may be supporting points, but they are not elaborated upon. Some of the details may be irrelevant to the topic, purpose, or audience.

1 = NOVICE
The main idea of the essay is implicit but not clear. There tend to be too few or no supporting points and the details presented tend not to be elaborated upon. Some of the details or elaboration may be irrelevant to the topic, purpose, or audience.

Exercise 1: Opinions and Ideas

Give your opinion of the following questions; state your answer as a possible main idea of an essay.

1. Should the school day be lengthened? Shortened?

Example: The school day should be shortened because it is too tiring for young people.

2. Is athletic ability learned or inherited?

3. Is artistic talent learned or inherited?

4. How well does your school handle discipline?

5. What would you like to see as the next big technological breakthrough?

6. What book, movie, or play should your school add to the curriculum?

7. What book, movie, or play should your school *drop* from its curriculum?

8. Who in your school deserves to be honored as "Student of the Month"?

9. What invention or innovation has contributed most to the quality of your life?

10. What invention or innovation has actually made your life more *difficult*?

While everyone can, and does, have opinions, those held in highest regard are those for which supporting details are provided.

Exercise 2: Elaborating on Your Idea with Supporting Details

*Choose the idea from **Exercise 1** in which you have the most interest and the clearest understanding. Then, elaborate on that idea by considering the "5 W's and 1 H." First, consider all of the variations to each question your topic might involve, and then answer each variation.*

Who:

> *Example*: **Who** would benefit from shortening the school day?
>
> **Who** might be inconvenienced?
>
> **Who** has the authority to make such a change?
>
> **Who** would be the most effective advocate of this change?
>
> **Who** would be the most powerful opponent of this change?

What:

> *Example*: **What** benefits are there to shortening the school day?
>
> **What** might be some of the disadvantages?
>
> **What** other impacts would this change have?
>
> > • on the remainder of the school day?
> >
> > • on people's schedules?

Where:

> *Example*: **Where** would students go after school?

When:

> *Example*: **When** would a change like this take place?
>
> **When** would school dismiss on a shortened day?

Why:

> *Example*: **Why** would this be a good change?
>
> **Why** are the listed benefits benefits?
>
> **Why** are the listed disadvantages disadvantages?
>
> **Why** would supporters support this change?
>
> **Why** would opponents oppose it?

How:

Example: **How** would you go about instituting this change?

How would this change affect:

- test scores, graduation requirements, acceptance to college?
- after-school jobs or participation in non-school activities?

Note: Some of the questions seem to repeat information you've already collected, and some indicate information you probably will not use in your final essay. This is fine. At this stage, your purpose is to get as much information as you can, and to examine that information from many different points of view. There will be time to eliminate duplicated and irrelevant information later. Right now, do not exclude anything you think of as "useless." Just jot it down and keep brainstorming.

Exercise 3: Developing Ideas from other Content Areas

Consider what you are currently studying in your other academic classes and do the following:

Note an idea or concept you've studied this week with which you agree.

Note an idea or concept you've studied this week with which you disagree.

Note an idea or concept you've studied this week which you find especially interesting.

Note an idea or concept you've studied this week that you do not fully understand.

For the idea or concept with which you agree, answer the following questions:

How much do you know about this subject?

What is the basis of your agreement?

What evidence can you offer to support your opinion?

What evidence exists to support the opposite opinion?

How can you refute that evidence?

For the idea or concept you find particularly interesting, answer the following questions:

Is this new knowledge or something you knew before?

What do you find interesting about it?

What background information would you have to give to a reader in order to explain this?

Using Modes of Development to Develop Ideas

There are four main *purposes* for writing: to inform, to persuade, to express personal feelings and opinions, and to entertain. We will further discuss these purposes later in the series.

The *purpose* for each piece of writing has many implications for the level and type of development of the ideas in the essay and for the organization of the essay; therefore, there will be times when we will discuss purpose under development and others when we will discuss purpose under organization.

When discussing purpose as part of development, it is helpful to describe the several *modes of development.* These, quite simply, specify the *type* of information, the *kind* of details you will need to achieve your purpose.

The following are the six key modes of development:

1. **Description** deals with the *physical* details of an object: size, shape, color, texture, smell, taste, etc. Using description to develop an idea implies an awareness of *spatial order* or *order of magnitude* (from most important to least important or vice versa).

    Developing your topic by providing physical details can play an important role in all four of the purposes for writing:
    *   informing your reader of something's nature
    *   persuading your reader of one thing's superiority over another
    *   expressing an opinion about the quality of something
    *   establishing setting or characterization for a piece of fiction, memoir, personal statement, etc.

2. **Narration** deals with a *sequence of events*, actions and reactions. Use of narration implies an awareness of *chronological order* (or reverse chronological order).

    Developing your topic by narrating the events will come in most handy when you need to:
    *   inform your reader of essential background (what happened before, the history or development of something, etc.)
    *   persuade your reader of some future consequence (based on an understanding of past events)
    *   tell a story.

    It is important to note, however, that there are times when you will be strongly tempted to narrate a story's plot or an author's biography when this information is *not relevant* to your topic. You do not need to summarize an entire novel to discuss the symbolism of a particular image. You do not need to give a step-by-step description of a family vacation to evaluate how that vacation brought you closer to your siblings.

3. **Illustration** develops your ideas by providing examples. Sometimes the examples can come in the form of similes and metaphors. The use of illustration most likely involves *order of magnitude* (best example to least or vice versa).

Again, illustration can be useful for writing in each of the four purposes:

- informing your reader of something's nature by providing examples rather than struggling to describe it
- persuading your reader how similar (or different) two things are by providing examples of each
- using an example, especially a simile or metaphor, to express a mood or feeling that is difficult to express in another way
- creating an entire story as an example of a point you want to establish or a lesson you want to teach your reader.

4. **Process,** like narration, deals with a *sequence of events.* The key difference between the two is that process is a narrower, more focused sequence, usually with a specific end result in mind. Process will almost always employ *chronological order.*

Process is most helpful when

- informing your reader how to do something
- persuading your reader that there is an easier or more efficient way of doing something.

5. **Classification** deals with groups and categories, what things have in common and how they belong together. Classification differs from description in that it leads the reader to certain conclusions about the value of the characteristics described. The use of classification implies *order of magnitude* or possibly *spatial order.*

Classification is also narrower and more focused than description in that you will provide your reader *with only* those traits relevant to the category in which you are placing the object you are classifying.

Classification is most useful in *informative* writing, but might also be used in

- persuading your reader to view something in a particular way
- expressing your view of something by the category in which you place it.

6. **Definition** is also similar to description but deals with non-physical attributes as well as physical details. For example, whereas your description of a particular chair would most likely include color, size, material, etc., your definition of "a chair" would need to include its *purpose.*

Definition is useful when you need to
- inform your reader of a new term or object or clarify your particular use of a term
- persuade your reader of the presence (or absence) of some trait (e.g., there is no justice in the court system) by carefully defining what you mean by that trait
- express your feelings about some abstract concept (love, honor, etc.).

Exercise 4: Exploring Modes of Development

Consider the opinion questions that you answered in Exercise 1. For each, list the mode(s) of development you would need to use to discuss your response to that question. Also list some of the details you would include for each mode of development:

1. Should the school day be lengthened? Shortened?

Example:
Description of overworked student:
Narration: step-by-step description of a typical school day, emphasizing how long and tiring it is
Classification: symptoms of overwork, description of problems associated with overwork
Illustration: examples of schools or districts with shorter school days; case studies of students with problems due to length of school day

2. Is athletic ability learned or inherited?

3. Is artistic talent learned or inherited?

4. How well does your school handle discipline?

5. What would you like to see as the next big technological breakthrough?

6. What book, movie, or play should your school add to the curriculum?

7. What book, movie, or play should your school *drop* from its curriculum?

8. Who in your school deserves to be honored as "Student of the Month"?

9. What invention or innovation has contributed most to the quality of your life?

10. What invention or innovation has actually made your life more *difficult*?

Brainstorming Details by Association/Clustering

You are probably familiar with the graphic organizer called the "web" or the "cluster," a popular tool for generating details.

Let's review your use and expand on your understanding of this tool so you can use it more effectively.

Begin with a general topic, such as cooking. Then, narrow it, for example: famous culinary schools.

Then, ask yourself, "What about it?" Write the phrase or sentence that answers, "What about it?" in the center of your cluster. This is your **main idea**, and may even be your **thesis statement** if you write it as a complete sentence.

Next, fill in bubbles around your main idea with supporting ideas, or **sub-points**, that prove it.

Finally, add bubbles around these sub-points, or ideas, that contain examples and explanations, also called supporting **details**. Your objective is to prove the point you make in the center of the cluster, your main idea.

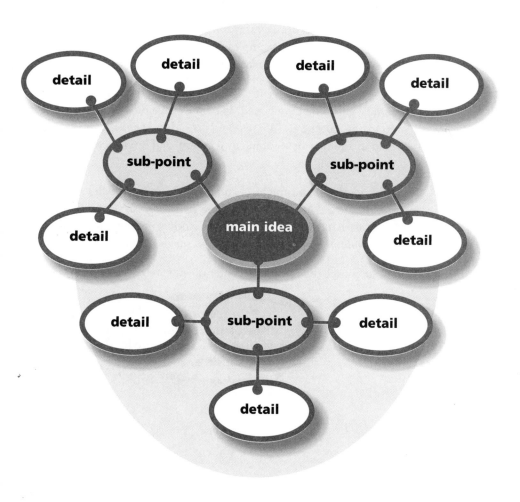

Study the following example:

The topic is professional athletes. In bubbles, write some thoughts that come to mind.

Step 1: At the center of the web—as you probably already know—is your main idea. What you may not yet realize is that you *cannot state this main idea in a single word* or even in a single noun phrase.

Professional Athletes is not an essay topic, or a main idea. Neither is *Lance Armstrong.* These are both examples of general topics, which are too large to be covered properly in one paragraph.

When you consider the 1st Truth, "Powerful writing really says something," you should realize that your main idea must include at least a *hint* of an answer to the question, *"What about it?"* This *"what about it"* can be answered in a phrase or a complete sentence, and it will actually begin to help you shape your thesis.

So *Professional Athletes* might become *"Professional athletes have many opportunities to act like role models,"* and *Lance Armstrong* might become *"Cyclist Lance Armstrong established the Lance Armstrong Foundation and has raised millions for cancer research and survivor support."*

Write your complete topic in the center of your web:

Professional athletes have many opportunities to act like role models.

Step 2: You must have had some idea of what you meant when you thought up the words of your topic. So now, you can wrap some words around that. These are the sub-points. What do you mean when you say that professional athletes should conduct themselves as role models?

- Professional athletes serve as prime examples of fitness and healthy living.

- Many athletes establish charities and donate time and money to charitable events.

- The league, the team, and the media require athletes to demonstrate acceptable behavior

... and so on.

Add these ideas to your web:

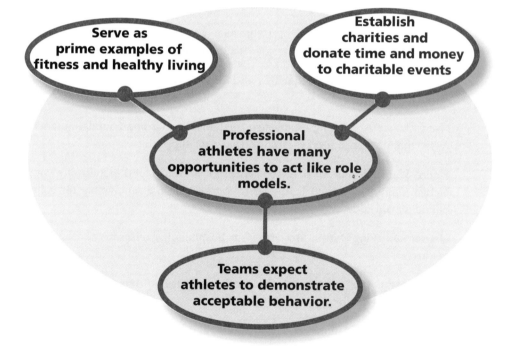

Step 3: Now, for each of these statements, you must have *at least three or four supporting details (e.g. illustrations, evidence, or examples).* If you have no supporting details, your point is simply not valid, and you must rethink it. If you turn in an essay that offers no examples, you will receive a well-deserved failing grade—not because your teacher disagrees with your opinion, but simply because you failed to support it.

So what examples can you offer for each of your sub-points?

- **Professional athletes serve as prime examples of fitness and healthy living.**

Through F3 (Food for Fuel) athletes visit schools to teach fitness and nutrition.

MLB's PLAY Campaign visits stadiums throughout the country and various MLB players teach kids about health concerns, healthy eating, and active living.

Before becoming governor of California, professional body builder Arnold Schwarzenegger chaired the President's Council on Physical Fitness.

- **Many athletes establish charities and donate time and money to charitable events.**

Cyclist Lance Armstrong established the Lance Armstrong Foundation and has raised millions for cancer research and survivor support.

Figure skater Michelle Kwan has been the spokeswoman for the Children's Miracle Network and has worked with Chevrolet to establish a scholarship for college-bound female athletes.

Detroit Red Wing Darren McCarty visits hospitals and raises money for medical research.

- **The league, the team, and the media require athletes to demonstrate acceptable behavior.**

NBA Cares donates money to various causes and encourages athletes and coaches to donate hours of service.

Minnesota Vikings' new owner had a new code of conduct written to outline the positive behavior expected of players on and off the field.

Former Philadelphia Eagle Terrell Owens' highly publicized inappropriate behavior resulted in suspension and deactivation for the remainder of the season.

Through F3 (Food for Fuel) athletes visit schools to teach fitness and nutrition.

Figure skater Michelle Kwan has been the spokeswoman for the Children's Miracle Network and has worked with Chevrolet to establish a scholarship for college-bound female athletes.

MLB's PLAY Campaign visits stadiums throughout the country, and various MLB players teach kids about health concerns, healthy eating, and active living.

Cyclist Lance Armstrong established the Lance Armstrong Foundation and has raised millions for cancer research and survivor support.

Detroit Red Wing Darren McCarty visits hospitals and raises money to find a cure for a specific type of cancer.

Serve as prime examples of fitness and healthy living

Establish charities and donate time and money to charitable events

Professional athletes have many opportunities to act like role models.

Before becoming governor of California, professional body builder Arnold Schwarzenegger chaired the President's Council on Physical Fitness.

NBA Cares donates money to various causes and encourages athletes and coaches to donate hours of service.

Teams expect athletes to demonstrate acceptable behavior.

Former Philadelphia Eagle Terrell Owens' highly publicized inappropriate behavior resulted in suspension and deactivation for the remainder of the season.

Minnesota Vikings' new owner had a new code of conduct written to outline the positive behavior expected of players on and off the field.

Step 4: Of course, while you're generating ideas and supporting details for your well-developed and elaborated essay, you'll realize that your step three sub-points can be developed still further. For example, the statement that athletes visit schools to teach fitness and nutrition through F3 *demands* a few details about which athletes and which schools. And if you *really* want to write powerfully, you'll also explain how those athletes teach their message and how and why they choose the schools they visit.

Does this mean that you can divide a sub-point into details and sub-details *ad infinitum*? Actually, it does. The only factors you need to take into consideration in determining how deeply you will delve into your topic are how much time you have to write the essay or paper, and the page limit you've been assigned.

Since you should develop even a one-page essay as fully as possible, these factors have much more impact on your selection of topic. This will be discussed later.

Exercise 5: Brainstorming Ideas

Choose one of the topics you created in Exercise 1, and brainstorm as many sub-points and developing details as you can. Represent the relationships between your ideas in a web.

Exercise 6: Brainstorming Ideas

Choose another one of the topics you created in Exercise 1, and brainstorm as many sub-points and developing details as you can. This time, experiment with your own outline or graphic organizer form to represent the relationships between these ideas.

Writing Opportunity: *The Essay Exam*

THROUGHOUT YOUR ACADEMIC CAREER, you will be required to demonstrate in writing what you have learned in class. Frequently, this will be part of an exam administered under time constraints.

While *all* of the traits of powerful essays are important, Development and Elaboration is the most important. Because the purpose of an essay question on an exam is to demonstrate what you have learned, you won't do that very well if you fail to provide specific detail and offer plenty of examples from your reading, class discussion, and teacher lecture.

The following writing prompt is similar to ones you are likely to encounter in a history class and a geography class. We have kept it as general as possible so everyone can write the essay(s) from his or her own knowledge. Choose one and answer the question in an essay.

Apply the techniques you have learned in this chapter to generate specific details in support of your main idea. You do want to get an A on this exam, and you can only do that by really impressing your teacher with how much you have learned.

Prompt: *Choose an important figure from United States history and explain the role he or she played.*

Step 1: *Choose your topic*
What historical person do you know the most about? Which one will provide you with the most specific ideas to write about?

Step 2: *Draft your main idea*
Previously, you learned that a thesis, or main idea, cannot be stated in a single word, but must at least *hint* at the answer to the question, "What about it?"

If you answer the "what about it" in a single sentence, you probably will have generated a main idea and the beginning of your thesis. Thinking about your topic in these terms really lets you take control of the topic and lets you focus on everything you *do* know.

Also, since you will probably not be able to discuss *everything* about your topic in the time and space allowed (usually an hour or so and a page or two), your main idea allows you to narrow your topic down to those aspects you best understand.

Time Clue: In a typical exam setting, you will have in the area of 2 hours for the entire exam. That means you might have one hour or less to write your essay. Assuming you have an hour for this essay, you should spend no more than 5 minutes thinking of a topic and main idea. Remember, you do want to show your teacher how much you know, so the main idea will probably come from the course content.

Step 3: *Brainstorm and generate ideas and supporting details*
Answer the 5 W's and 1 H. Think about aspects of your topic with which you agree and those with which you disagree. List facts or ideas. Think about the sensory details that might help you elaborate on your topic. Create a graphic organizer to help you generate new ideas and begin to organize them.

Time Clue: If you have one hour to work on your essay, allow yourself 10 – 15 minutes for Step 3.

Step 4: *Freewrite your first draft*
Make it as good as you can. This is a freewrite. You have already generated your details, so this is organizing them and explaining them to your reader. Depending on how much time you have for your essay, this might be your only draft—so make it good.

Time Clue: Give yourself 20 – 30 minutes for this step. If you did a good enough job in Step 3, writing the essay will be a breeze.

Step 5: *Revise and rewrite*

Set your draft aside for a minute or two. Then read it over and look especially for "holes" in the information. Are you really telling your teacher *everything* you know about the topic? Are you offering specific details? You also want to pay some attention to grammar, mechanics, spelling, and so on.

If you have time, you may actually want to create a new, clean draft of the paper, or you may simply make your *legible* corrections on your first draft.

Step 6: *Turn in your exam*

3 Simple Truths and 6 Essential Traits of Powerful Writing

Applying
the
Second Truth

Powerful writing is understandable to others.

3
Simple Truths
and
6
Essential Traits
of

Powerful Writing

Organization

Trait
Two

TRAIT TWO:
ORGANIZATION

ALL *GOOD* WRITING IS ORGANIZED. The organizational plan might be so subtle that the audience is not aware of being led from one point to the next and finally to a conclusion, b u t if the journey from the beginning to the conclusion has made sense to the reader, then the piece is organized.

The question, then, is how to create this organization. The secret is to know your options and to choose one.

> When we talk about organization, we are actually talking about two separate but related issues:
> - the organization of the entire essay,
> - and the organization of the individual sub-points within the essay.

Make Yours Better!

Note that the basic lack of Organization in this essay makes it difficult to read and follow.

During the winter in many parts of the United States, there are people who go to work in the dark and come home in the dark. Doctors have found this lack of sunlight can cause people to become depressed.

The Alaska pipeline becomes the focal point in the city. More than 5,000 people work on the pipeline. The greatest challenge these workers face is the around-the-clock work. The stress and little opportunity for vacationing contribute to the depression of people in Anchorage, Alaska.

Natives of this oil pipeline city find winters hard. People who have grown up in Alaska are a little more used to the short days, but it is a real problem for people new to the state. The condition is called Seasonal Affective Disorder (SAD), and there are a number of therapies available for it. Winter is a tough time for animals as well. Unlighted roadways present a big hazard, and even large animals like moose are killed by motorists who do not see them on the road until it is too late. Of course, the roads through most of Alaska are far too long and remote to even consider the possibility of installing street lights. Plus, the cost of keeping these lights on for over twenty hours a day for months on end would be enormous.

- No sub-points suggest how the point will be developed.

- The second paragraph discusses a new point instead of developing what has been introduced. This sudden change without a transition into a discussion of the pipeline is jarring to the reader.

- This tangent about animals and the installation of street lights is not related to the topic of depression.

Here the essay offers good discussion about the causes and treatment of SAD, but this information belongs in the previous paragraph where the disorder and available therapies are introduced.

This information on the sun, the solstices, etc., should be moved closer to the introduction where it will serve as explanatory background information. Additionally, the economic consequences of depression should be mentioned in the introduction as a sub-point.

As a conclusion, this paragraph is randomly organized, just like the details of this essay. It does not arrive at any strong conclusion, just as the introduction does not establish the main point and how it is going to be explored.

Most people who live in Alaska suffer from depression during these short days and long nights. Just as the animals go into hibernation, these sunlight-deprived people sleep most of the day. One of the causes of Seasonal Affective Disorder is that light controls the release of melatonin in the brain, and people who get depressed in the winter do not have enough melatonin. Many people find the use of special lights that imitate sunlight to be very helpful in treating SAD.

The sun is such a distance from the equator that people and animals see little sunlight. They are not productive and often suffer disastrous economic consequences. In fact, more people go bankrupt in Alaska than in any other state in the union.

The winter solstice is when the sun is at its southern-most point. The earth does not orbit the sun in a flat circle, but in a wobbly oval that makes the sun appear to move north and south over the earth as the year progresses. Regions to the far north—like Alaska, Russia, and Scandinavia—receive fewer and fewer hours of sunlight as the sun "moves" farther south. The sunlight these regions do receive is very weak, with the sun staying close to the horizon. North of the Arctic Circle, there is a period of up to six months when the sun never rises above the horizon at all.

The sunlight is found south of the equator. On the winter solstice—December 22—the sun is the farthest south of the equator that it will be all year. Therapists report that they cannot treat all the people who are suffering from depression. During this dark time in Alaska, people who work on the pipeline work up to 24-hour days. These unfortunate people go to work in the dark and come home from work in the dark. There is no possible way to live in Anchorage, Alaska, without experiencing the darkness of depression.

Essay Critique

This essay contains some relevant information that could be interesting and helpful to the reader. The writer has obviously done some research to understand the causes of SAD, its treatments, and the reasons for the prevalence of winter depression in places like Anchorage, Alaska. The biggest problem is that the information is presented randomly. The organization problem begins in the introduction where there is neither a clear main point nor a suggestion of how this point is going to be explored.

This essay receives a score of 1 on the:

Organization Rubric

5 = The organizational plan of the essay is clear and consistently applied but is obvious and/or formulaic (e.g., the five-paragraph essay), thus limiting the essay's overall effectiveness.

4 = DEVELOPING
An appropriate but obvious organizational plan is apparent and generally followed, but jumps or gaps distract the reader.

3 = An organizational plan is apparent but followed inconsistently so that the reader may be distracted by jumps or gaps. The apparent plan may not be the most appropriate for the topic, purpose, or audience.

2 = An organizational plan is suggested, but the overall effect of the essay seems more intuitive or accidental than intentional. Deviations from the plan are unintentional and distracting. The apparent plan may not be the most appropriate for the topic, purpose, or audience.

1 = NOVICE
The essay lacks an intentional organizational plan. Ideas are presented simply as they occurred to the writer.

The Basic Five-Paragraph Essay[1]

The five-paragraph essay is a traditional, clear-cut method of organizing an essay. It provides a strong model of organization.

Paragraph 1 is your INTRODUCTION. State as briefly as possible the main point of your essay and all of the major sub-points you are going to discuss, in the order you will address them. You should aim for three sub-points.

Paragraphs 2, 3, and 4 are your BODY PARAGRAPHS. Each paragraph restates a different sub-point from your introduction (in the order in which they appear in the introduction) and elaborates on it with facts, explanations, examples, and so forth.

Paragraph 5 is your CONCLUSION. Here, you wrap up the information you've presented in your body paragraphs, and show how you have made your essay's main point.

Essentially, what the five-paragraph essay does for the NOVICE and DEVELOPING writer is to ensure that you have a clear and pointed introduction, a body that really does elaborate on the introduced points, and a conclusion that clarifies the point for your reader.

---

[1]At the NOVICE and DEVELOPING levels, we strongly recommend that you master the basic five-paragraph essay format. As you ascend the scale and reach the PROFICIENT and ACCOMPLISHED levels, you will discover more sophisticated ways to organize your essays and longer papers.

Sample Five-Paragraph Essay

Peter Samuels is the best candidate for President of the Student Council for a number of reasons. First of all, Peter is reliable. If he says he will do something, I'm confident he will do it. Secondly, Peter is a hard worker. He won't give up easily, even if the task turns out to be harder than he thought it was going to be. Finally, Peter will not allow the "in crowd" to pressure him to do things. For all of these reasons, I think Peter Samuels will be the best president our Student Council has ever had.

> ▨ Introduction of main point (Peter Samuels is best candidate) and three sub-points (honest, hard-working, unpopular.)

Peter is one of the most honest people I know. Just last week we were all studying for our math mid-term. If you know Peter at all, you know that math is his worst subject. The only reason he is passing at all is that I tutor him every day after school and walk him step-by-step through all of the problems. Well, someone in our math class found a copy of the mid-term exam on Mr. L—'s desk and photocopied it for everyone. Not only did Peter refuse to cheat on the exam, he told Mr. L— who, exactly, stole the exam and which students had taken copies. That's how honest he is.

> ▨ Elaboration of the first sub-point (Peter is honest), using the specific example of the stolen exam.

Peter is also a hard worker. I've never known him to give up on anything he has ever attempted. When we were in elementary school together, Peter could not read, and the teacher asked me to help him. We sat at his desk through every recess, lunch hour, and even after school working our way through the book. It was hard work. Peter would often look out the window at the other boys and girls playing on the swings and monkey bars, but he never once thought about quitting and playing. By the end of the year, he was pretty much caught up with everyone in the class. Since he really has no other activity to take up his time, I know he will be just as hard a worker as Student Council President.

> ▨ Elaboration of the second sub-point (Peter is hard-working), using the specific example of learning to read.

But probably the most important characteristic of Peter's that will make him an excellent choice for president is that he is unpopular. I am pretty much his only friend. Now, you might think that this would be a handicap in a student election, but what it really means is that Peter will not be swayed to do "cool" things just because the popular kids want it. A lot of the girls and health-nuts in class have been complaining that they want a salad bar in the cafeteria for lunch. Peter does not like salad, and since these complainers are not his friends anyway, he won't feel pressured to fight for a salad bar just because "they" want it. His lack of friends lets him be his own person.

> ▨ Elaboration of the third sub-point (Peter is unpopular) with the specific example of a salad bar.

So Peter Samuels is the best choice for Student Council President. He is honest, hard-working, and independent. No one else can make these claims, so I urge you to vote for Peter next Thursday.

> ▨ Conclusion reiterates the three sub-points that have been discussed and restates the main point.

Examining the Basic Principles of Organization

Having established an organizational pattern for your essay, next you must organize the information *within* the essay. This is *your choice as writer of the essay,* but there are two important considerations you must factor into your decision:

- **What does the topic demand?**

  Often the topic of the essay dictates how the material is to be organized. For example, a simple narrative about an experience or event would probably make best sense when written chronologically; likewise, a process, or how-to, essay would also have to be written sequentially, or else it would make no sense at all. In an argumentative or persuasive essay, you might decide to present your material either from most convincing to least convincing or from least to most. A physical description of an object or place would most likely require some sort of spatial plan: front to back, top to bottom, etc.

- **What will your audience need?**

  Every piece of writing has an audience (for example: parents, friends, opponents, etc.). The best writers consider their audience as they compose their work and write with that audience in mind. Even if the essay you are writing is an assignment to be read only by your teacher, you *will* have an idea of who "your audience" is. Meeting the needs of the audience is a large factor in determining if writing is poor, adequate, or good. Knowing who your audience is (age, level of education, amount of knowledge in your subject) will help you determine what type of information you need to present, how much, and in what order.

Types of Organization

Chronological Order:
In narrative writing, this is basic order of organization according to time: this happened first, then this happened, and then this happened. In *process*, or *how-to*, essays, chronological order lays out the first step, and explains the process, step-by-step. *Cause and effect* essays establish that *effects* follow *causes*, and so on.

Spatial Order:
When writing a descriptive essay, you need to establish some sort of spatial organization, whether it is top to bottom, left to right, or front to back. Be sure that your method is consistent and appropriate for your subject. For example, when describing a person, your reader will be better able to visualize the subject if you depict the person from head to toe. Your reader might lose track if you change direction. If you begin with top-to-bottom description, you need to stick to this organization. The same applies if you use side-to-side description. Switching directions may confuse your reader.

Order of Importance:
Here you'll decide whether it would be better to discuss your most important, most convincing points first and work your way to the least, or *vice versa.* There will be times when either pattern will work effectively. Much of your choice depends on what you believe will make the most sense to your particular audience. *However, once you make your decision, you must be consistent.* Order of importance also includes definition essays in which you start with a general rule and then discuss specific examples, and those in which you show specific examples and use them to establish a general rule.

Alternating Comparison:
When writing a comparison/contrast essay, focus on the *objects* or *concepts* being compared and discuss all of the traits of one and then all of the traits of the other.

For example:

Apples	Oranges
– no need to peel—eat "as is"	– difficult to peel
– high in fiber (more filling)	– juicy (less filling)
– local varieties available most places	– grow only in warm locations

Exercise 1: Choosing the Best System of Organization

Consider each of the following writing topics and prompts and write which of the above organizational patterns would probably serve you best.

- Your school board is considering rescinding the privilege of driving to school, and you have been assigned to write an article for the school newspaper explaining the many advantages of riding the school bus.

  Organizational Pattern: _____

- Your history teacher has assigned you an essay in which you are to compare the presidencies of George Bush and his son, George W. Bush.

  Organizational Pattern: _____

- You witnessed the beginning of a food fight in the cafeteria and have been asked to write an incident report in which you tell what you saw.

  Organizational Pattern: _____

- An essay question on a final exam asks you to support *either* Darwin's theory of evolution *or* the theory of intelligent design.

  Organizational Pattern: _____

- You have been assigned to write the current school year's "recap" for your school's yearbook.

  Organizational Pattern: _____

- The prom committee is considering two possible locations for this year's prom, and you decide to write to the committee chairperson recommending the site you think would be better.

  Organizational Pattern: _____

Writing and Using an Outline

Whenever you hear the word "outline," what probably pops into your mind is the academic outline with Roman numerals, Arabic numerals, and upper and lower case letters. If you're like most novice writers, you probably understand the rules and format of the outline more than its actual use. While the mechanics of outlining using Roman numerals, capital letters, etc., are well known, many students do not realize that an outline can be and is a *very* useful tool in writing a well-organized essay. We will briefly review the elements and principles of an outline, and then examine the "rules" by looking at how an outline operates.

Each level of notation (Roman numeral, upper case letter, Arabic numeral, lower case level) represents a particular "size" of the idea noted there:

- Roman numerals (I, II, III) are the main ideas you want to establish in your essay.
  - Upper case letters (A, B, C) are the sub-points into which you can divide your main ideas.
    - Arabic numerals (1, 2, 3) are supporting details.
      - Lower case letters (a, b, c) are explanations of details.
        - And so on.

The indentation formula allows you to *see* the relationship between the main ideas, and the various levels of sub-points under each main idea. In this way, an outline lets you *visually* keep track of your ideas and their relationship to each other *before* you try to express them in paragraph form.

I.
  A.
    1.
      a.
      b.
    2.
      a.
      b.
  B.
    1.
      a.
      b.
    2.
      a.
      b.

II.
  A.
    1.
      a.
      b.
    2.
      a.
      b.
  B.
    1.
      a.
      b.
    2.
      a.
      b.

You cannot have only one item at a particular level. Think of it this way:

- Your Roman numerals are the main "parts" of your topic.
  - The upper case letters are the "parts" of the Roman numeral under which you've placed them.
    - The Arabic numerals are "parts" of the upper case letters, and so on.

Then remember that *you cannot break something into only one part!* So, for every "**I**" you need a "**II**;" for every "**A**" you need a "**B**;" for every "**1**" you need a "**2**;" and so on.

In the Sample Five-Paragraph Essay on page 37, the topic is Peter Samuels as the best candidate for President. The three main points (Roman numerals) are as follows:

I.   he's honest;
II. he's a hard worker; and
III. he's unpopular.

Now, if the *only* point you were going to develop were that he's honest, that would *not* be (I). It would be your *topic*, which you would then divide into two or more main ideas to create an entirely different five-paragraph essay.

Peter Samuels is honest.
I.   main idea 1
II. main idea 2
III. main idea 3

It is also important that you strive to develop every part of your topic to the same level. In outline terms, that means if you go to the lower-case-letter level in one section, you should make a concerted effort to go that deep in all of your sections. By describing one aspect of your topic in full detail and then glossing over another with barely a mention, you create a very uneven essay.

Using Your Outline to Diagnose Problems Before You Write the Essay

If you develop the habit of thinking about your outline as an essential step in the writing, you will find that having a well thought-out outline can help you with the two essential traits of Development and Elaboration and Organization.

Scenario 1: The Underdeveloped Essay

If—after you've done everything you can to generate ideas and supporting details— you cannot take your outline deeper than the Roman numeral or upper-case-letter level, your essay will be **underdeveloped.** Before you even write your first draft, you **must** rethink your topic, change your focus, brainstorm more ideas, research more facts, and so on. You can*not* simply write the essay because you do not have enough information, support, and details to do so. The essay would lack sufficient development and elaboration.

Scenario 2: The Overdeveloped Essay

On the other hand, if you find yourself with more than five or six main ideas (V or VI), or more than four or five sub-points (D or E), or more than five or six details (5 or 6), then your essay will be **overdeveloped.** This means that your topic itself is too broad, and you must narrow your focus. It may also mean that some of the information you gathered in the earlier steps is irrelevant to your topic.

Scenario 3: The Unevenly Developed Essay

In the same way, if you find more than five or six details in some areas of your outline, but other areas are not developed beyond the Roman numeral or upper case letter, then your essay will be **unevenly developed.** You need to rethink the focus of your topic, possibly emphasizing areas where you have more information. Some of the overdeveloped parts of the outline might contain irrelevant information.

But in all three of the above scenarios, the depth of your outline offers you an excellent preview of the quality of the essay you are about to write, and provides you with the chance to fix an essay that would most likely receive a low or failing grade.

Exercise 2: Recognizing a Problem Outline

Indicate the problem, if any, with the essays that would develop from each of the following outlines:

Topic 1
I. Main idea
   A. sub-point
     1. detail
     2. detail
     3. detail
     4. detail
     5. detail
     6. detail
   B. sub-point
     1. detail
     2. detail
     3. detail
     4. detail
     5. detail
     6. detail
II. Main idea
   A. sub-point
     1. detail
     2. detail
     3. detail
     4. detail
     5. detail
     6. detail
   B. sub-point
     1. detail
     2. detail
     3. detail
     4. detail

Problem: _____

Topic 2
I. Main idea
   A. sub-point
     1. detail
     2. detail
     3. detail
     4. detail
     5. detail
     6. detail
   B. sub-point
II. Main idea
   A. sub-point
   B. sub-point
     1. detail
     2. detail

Problem: _____

Topic 3
I. Main idea
   A. sub-point
   B. sub-point
II. Main idea
   A. sub-point
   B. sub-point

Problem: _____

Exercise 3: Creating an Outline

Choose something you've discussed in one of your classes (such as historical figures, current events, sportsmanship, etc.) and formulate an essay topic. Use some of the strategies you learned in Chapter One to generate ideas. Then, outline your essay, paying close attention to the rules discussed under the heading **Writing and Using an Outline** *on page 41.*

Exercise 4: Using a Web to Create an Outline

Choose one of the topics listed in Exercise 1, on page 40, and generate ideas using a web. Then, outline your main ideas and sub-points.

Exercise 5: Experimenting with Organization

Choose one of the topics from Exercise 1 of this chapter or from Exercise 1 of Chapter One on page 13.

- *Use some of the strategies you learned in Chapter One and generate ideas.*

- *Outline the essay you would write, applying what you learned in this chapter.*

- *Copy each separate line onto an index card without the Roman numeral, upper-case letter, etc. notation.*

- *Rearrange the cards and experiment with different orders of ideas and groupings of main ideas, sub-points, etc.*

- *Consider the benefits and disadvantages of each order/grouping.*

- *Finally, select the one you think will work best for you in communicating your ideas.*

- *Write a few brief, informal paragraphs about why this particular grouping/ order will work better than the others you tried.*

Exercise 6: Using an Outline to Correct an Essay

*Outline the **Make Yours Better** essay on page 33. Remember that your Roman numerals represent main points of development, not individual paragraphs.*

- *Copy each line from your outline onto index cards without the outline notation (I, A, 1, etc.).*

- *Rearrange the cards and experiment with different orderings and groupings as you did in Exercise 5.*

- *After you have arrived at the ordering and grouping of ideas that you think will make the most powerful essay, re-write the essay.*

- *Write a few brief, informal paragraphs about why the grouping/ordering you chose is more effective than the original order.*

Writing Opportunity: *The Homework Essay: Book Review*

A book review does not, as many students think, consist of a summary of the plot and descriptions of the book's characters and settings. Rather, a genuine book review involves an *evaluation* of the book and your *justification* for that evaluation. If you like the book, you must examine what you like about the book. If you do not like the book, you must explain why. If you think the book is particularly well-suited to certain readers, you must explore how.

While *all* the traits of powerful essays are important in a book review, Organization is probably the most important. Remember, the purpose of the book review is for you to communicate to a reader whether or not the book about which you are writing is a good "read" and the reasons why. You'll have a number of different ideas you'll want to cover—both main ideas and supporting details—and the order in which you present those ideas will largely determine whether or not your reader appreciates your point.

Applying the techniques from this chapter creates an organizational plan that will clearly establish your focus and help the reader appreciate your point.

Step 1: *Choose your topic*

What book are you going to review? Make certain you know the book's full title, the author's full and correct name, and the genre (literary type) of the book.

Step 2: *Draft your main idea*

Remember that the main idea must begin to answer the question, "What about it?" so you need to write a single sentence that sums up your feelings about the book. Good writing is the result of good thinking.

> Example: *The Dante Club,* by Matthew Pearl, is a fascinating blend of history, suspense, and horror that takes the reader on an adventure that even your English teacher will enjoy.

This is your main idea, your thesis. Thinking about your topic in these terms enables you to take control and establish your focus for your reader from the very beginning. Every sentence that follows in the essay somehow relates to and elaborates on this statement.

Note that you absolutely want to avoid overly vague statements ("*The Dante Club* was a good book.") or sentences that don't establish any focus at all ("I just finished reading *The Dante Club.*").

Also, since you will probably not be able to discuss *everything* you liked or disliked about the book due to the space allowed (book reviews are often limited to a few paragraphs, 500 words or so), your main idea allows you to narrow your focus to those aspects that are most important.

> **Time Clue:** Assume you have a week to write your review after you have read the book. You should actually be thinking of this main idea sentence, or thesis statement, before you are fully finished with the book. Certainly you should devote no more than a few hours to it. Once you've read the book, you know whether or not to recommend it and why. If you don't, you probably need to choose another book.

Step 3: *Think about the aspects of the book you are going to discuss and jot them down to begin your outline*
Jot them down on index cards and experiment with different orders, deciding on one that is logical. Start your outline.

Step 4: *Flip through the book and write down the specific details that explain, support, and illustrate your main ideas and sub-points.*
Write these also on index cards and add them to your outline.

Time Clue: For a weeklong assignment, you can safely devote one or two days to this step. Remember that it will be better for you to have too much material at this point than too little. You can always edit out the details that turn out to be extraneous or irrelevant.

Step 5: *Write your first draft*
Since you have already generated your details and organized them into a logical order, your first draft should be fairly well organized and easy to write.

Time Clue: Less than one day.

Step 6: *Revise and rewrite*
Set your draft aside for at least a day. You need to be able to look at it with fresh eyes in order to revise it effectively. This means that, for a weeklong assignment, you need to build into your schedule a day when you will not work on the assignment.

Then read it over and look for holes in the information and gaps in the structure and organizational plan. Are you being absolutely clear about your judgment of the book? Are you offering specific details from the book to show what you mean about each of your claims? You also want to pay some attention to grammar, mechanics, spelling, and so on.

Use the scoring rubrics on pages 12 and 35 and make certain your essay demonstrates your mastery.

Show your draft to one or two other people and have them read it and rate it according to the rubrics.

Rewrite the draft, fixing any of the problems you found when you reread it, and those that others found when you asked them to read it.

Finally, create a new, clean draft of the paper.

Time Clue: You may have just one day left for this step, but if you've been careful thinking, planning, and drafting all along, this is plenty of time.

Step 7: *Turn in your book review.*

Trait Three
Sentence Structure and Variety

TRAIT THREE:
SENTENCE STRUCTURE AND VARIETY

ALL POWERFUL SENTENCES have two things in common: clarity and completeness of thought. In writing clear, complete sentences, it is important to:

- consider word choice carefully.
- observe grammatical and mechanical conventions.
- make the best of appropriate sentence structure.

Sentence variety is a means by which the writer helps the reader to understand which ideas are most important, which ideas support or explain other ideas, etc. Variety of sentence structures is also a part of style and voice.

Make Yours Better!

Note that incorrect Sentence Structure and a lack of Sentence Variety make this otherwise interesting and informative essay very difficult to read.

A mysterious event occurred in a remote area of Siberia. June of 1908. Scientists still debate the cause of the incident.

  A huge explosion occurred. It happened in a remote, mosquito-infested swamp near the Tunguska River in Siberia, Russia. The Evenki, a tribe of reindeer herders, lived in the area of the explosion. They were eyewitnesses. They described seeing a bright, white light streak across the sky. They claimed the object had a tail over 800 kilometers long. It made no noise as it passed overhead. Then they heard five explosions. The second explosion was the most powerful. The Evenki people sealed off the area. They believed it was bewitched. They were afraid the gods were angry with them.

  The explosion sent shock waves through the earth. Like earthquakes. That were recorded all over the world. When the bright ball of fire hit the earth. A huge shaft of fire shot several thousand feet in the air the huge fire was visible for hundreds of miles away. It immediately produced a hot wind. That scorched forests and burned towns. There was destruction as far as 375 miles from the point where the fireball hit. Shock waves were heard as far as 800 miles away. Dark clouds formed over the area. Russia had a strange rain. Black debris and soil particles. Dust particles were carried all over the world.

- Two simple sentences and a fragment make the first paragraph choppy. The paragraph might seem "complete," but there is no sense of a main point and how that point is to be developed.

- Many simple sentences make it difficult to explore relationships between ideas.

- The second paragraph begins to combine sentence fragments (incomplete sentences) with the string of simple sentences. The fragments cause the reader to pause and wonder what the writer is trying to say.

The fragment does not communicate a complete idea and might be a part of the sentence before it or after it. Some fragments simply provide information with no apparent connection to anything else in the paragraph.

■ Notice how the last sentence fragment, "Until 13 years later," actually makes the sentence to which it should be attached factually incorrect.

Other parts of the world reported strange events. For several days, people in Russia enjoyed extra-colorful sunsets and sunrises. Scandinavia, and Western Europe too. Nights were light like day in Eastern Siberia and Middle Asia the nights remained so bright. You could easily read a newspaper or a book. Magnetic storms like those produced by nuclear explosions. In the United States. Scientists at the Smithsonian Astrophysical Observatory and California's Mount Wilson Observatory reported that the air was a lot less clear for looking through their telescopes.

Scientists in Russia could not immediately investigate the event. The Russians felt other matters were more important. They were in the middle of a Revolution. The Russian Revolution. The first expedition to research event did not take place. Until 13 years later.

1921. An expedition led by Leonid Kulik, a member of the Russian Meteorological Institute. The expedition bravely fought their way to the site of the explosion. They had to battle dangerous, uncharted swamps. Huge swarms of mosquitoes. They were shocked at the complete destruction they found. Trees were leveled to the ground around where the fireball had hit. At the place where the fireball hit. Trees were still standing. But were completely stripped of leaves and branches. The team theorized that a meteorite caused the damage. They searched for fragments of the meteorite. None were ever found. They used magnetic probes. But not one trace of metal was ever found.

There are still many theories about what caused the huge explosion. Leonid Kulik suggested that a huge meteorite crashed into the area. A colleague of his suggested that the force must have been caused by a freak windstorm. Since no debris from a meteorite could be found. Others claim it was a black hole that fell to Earth some think a great ball of anti-matter crashed on Earth.

1946. A. Kasantsev, a Soviet science fiction writer, published a story. The story told of a nuclear-powered alien spacecraft exploding in a fiery crash in the Tunguska area. This made people interested again. Felix Zigel and Aleksey Zolotov found radioactivity at the place of the crash. They said it was a crashed alien spacecraft. Even though later radioactive surveys didn't prove anything. They were Soviet scientists.

■ The continuing string of simple sentences and fragments makes this paragraph confusing. It is very difficult for the reader to focus on the information because of incomplete sentences and the choppy start-stop rhythm of the simple sentences.

Modern-day researchers believe a meteor or comet was responsible. But it exploded in mid air. Instead of actually crashing into Earth. They think. The diameter must have been around 200 yards. If the object were a meteor. The debris they couldn't find was overlooked. Or had vaporized in the explosion. Or possibly 'skipped' off the face of the Earth and shot back into space. Like skipping rocks off a pond. If the object had been an icy comet, then the debris simply melted. If an alien spacecraft had been the cause, then perhaps the debris had been recovered.

Scientists still wonder about some of the strange biological results of the event. Living things grow much faster in the center of the crash site than anywhere else. This rapid growth continues. To this day. Mutant species have been found too. Not just at the point of contact. But all along the path of the fireball. Over the Tunguska region. There have been strange mutations in the Evenki tribe. Most of the mutations to plant and animal life have never been explained.

What we do know for sure is that in 1908, something struck the Earth with a force of 40 megatons of TNT. 2,000 times the force of the atomic bomb that exploded over Hiroshima. We are very lucky. The event occurred in a remote area of Siberia. Continued investigation of this event is important. So we can be assured that another event of this size will never occur in the future.

Essay Critique

This essay is actually quite informative and fairly well organized. But the lack of sentence variety—every complete sentence is a simple sentence—and the significant number of sentence fragments make the essay very difficult to read. This format obscures much of the information and organization.

This essay receives a score of ❶ on the:

Sentence Structure Rubric

5 = There is an attempt to vary sentence length and structure, but it appears to be variety for variety's sake rather than topic, purpose, audience, and voice determining appropriate sentence structure. Minor problems in structure, grammar, and/or word choice make them less effective than they might be. These errors can be corrected with minor revision (insertion of words, creation of appositives and/or subordinate clauses, etc.).

4 = DEVELOPING
There is evidence of experimentation with sentence variety, but this variety is forced and may result in awkward and inappropriate constructions.

3 = Basic sentence formation (simple sentence, compound sentence) is accurate. There is an attempt to experiment with more sophisticated structures (complex, compound-complex sentences). Problems in structure may create convoluted sentences that require substantial revision (number agreement, rearrangement of phrases and clauses to make a fragment a sentence, etc.) to correct.

2 = Sentences are complete and structured correctly, but there is little or no variety in sentence structure.

❶ = NOVICE
There is little or no variety in sentence structure. Some sentence structure errors (fragments, run-ons) indicate a lack of control.

Examining How Sentences Work:
The Basic Sentence

Although a sentence can be as short as one word, *every well-crafted English sentence* contains at least *two* parts:
- a **subject** and
- a *verb*.

John *ran.*   **The bull** *charged.*   **People in political office** *vote.*

The *imperative sentence*, or command, shows simply the *verb* (or verb phrase). The **subject** is understood to be "you."
This type of sentence is often called the "you understood" sentence.

(You) *Go!*   **(You)** *Stay!*   **(You)** *Sit down!*

NOTE: In the above samples, the verb is capitalized because it is actually the first word in the sentence.
The "you" is in parenthesis because it is not explicitly stated when the command is spoken or written.
It is shown here only to illustrate that it is the assumed or understood subject of the sentence.

What Makes a Sentence Complete?

No sentence in the English language is a complete sentence unless it contains a subject and a predicate (or a "you-understood" subject in an imperative sentence). It is important to note that a subject and predicate alone usually will not make a sentence because a sentence must express a complete thought.

Note the following example:

John | threw
subject | *predicate*

This is not a complete thought; therefore, it is not a complete sentence. More information is necessary in order to complete the thought. We need to know what John threw.

Often the information necessary to complete the thought is contained in the predicate. The parts of the predicate that complete the meaning of the verb are collectively called "complements."

Note the following examples:

Incomplete:	Went to the store.
	*This is not a sentence because there is no subject.
Corrected:	**Mike** went to the store.
Incomplete:	Joan and her mother and her brothers.
	*This is not a sentence because there is no predicate.
Corrected:	Joan, her mother, and her brothers **went home.**
Incomplete:	Juanita saw.
	*Although there is a subject and predicate, this is not a complete sentence because the thought is not complete. In order for Juanita to see, she had to see <u>something</u>, and we do not yet know what she saw.
Corrected:	Juanita saw **a yellow bird in the tree.**

So, in addition to the subject and verb, most sentences must contain one or more of the following complements of the verb:

- direct objects,
- indirect objects,
- predicate nouns, or
- predicate adjectives.

Direct Objects

The *direct object* receives the action of the verb; in other words, the direct object is the person or thing being acted upon in the sentence. If John threw <u>*the ball,*</u> the ball is being acted upon. It is being thrown. Therefore, "the ball" is the direct object of the sentence.

John called <u>*Sally.*</u>
        DO

The bull charged <u>*Ramon.*</u>
        DO

Acid rain destroys <u>*plants and animals.*</u>
        DO

People in political office meet <u>*other people in political office.*</u>
        DO

Indirect Objects

The *indirect object* is the person or thing for whom the action is being performed. In the sentence "John threw *Mohandas* the ball," Mohandas is the indirect object, being the person for whom the ball was thrown. A sentence must have a direct object in order to have an indirect object.

> Substitute teachers teach *students* lessons.
>   IO   DO
>
> Juan gave *Miranda* a diamond ring.
>   IO   DO
>
> The gardener gave *the sunflowers* water.
>   IO   DO

Predicate Nouns

The *predicate noun* is a noun or pronoun that follows a linking verb[1] and renames subject of the verb. In the sentence "Janet is *class president*," class president is the predicate noun since it follows the linking verb (is) and renames the subject (Janet).

> Our English teacher is *Mrs. Jones*.
>   PN
>
> The man on the corner was *a renowned performer*.
>   PN
>
> Bubbles is *George's troublesome pet ferret*.
>   PN

Predicate Adjectives

The *predicate adjective* is an adjective that follows a linking verb and modifies the subject of the verb. In the sentence "Alex is *tall*," tall is the predicate adjective since it follows the linking verb (is) and modifies the subject (Alex).

> Bernie looked *exhausted*.
>   PA
>
> This steak tastes *delicious*.
>   PA
>
> Mother became *furious about the ink on the carpet*.
>   PA

---

[1]Linking verbs include the forms of *to be* (am, is, are, was, were, will be, being, been) and several other verbs that can be either action or linking depending on their use in the sentence. The most common of these verbs are *seem, grow, taste, smell, look, feel, sound, become, remain,* and *appear.*

Examining How Sentences Work: Modifiers and Objects

The simple subject and all its modifiers are collectively called the **subject** of the sentence; the verb and all of its complements (direct object, indirect object, predicate noun, and predicate adjective) are collectively called the **predicate** of the sentence.

A modifier is any word or phrase that clarifies, or modifies, the meaning of another word or phrase:

- **Adjectives** modify nouns;
- **Adverbs** modify verbs and adjectives.

> The _red_ ball rolled _slowly_ into the street.
>   ADJ   ADV

Red (adjective) tells something about the ball. _Slowly (adverb)_ tells something about how the ball rolled.

> The _tired and grumpy_ waitress sighed _sadly_ at the sight of the mess that
>   ADJ   ADV
> had been left for her to clean up.
>
> The _impatient, little_ child stared _excitedly_ at the person dressed in the
>   ADJ   ADV
> dinosaur costume.
>
> The _happy_ farmer was only _mildly_ happy.
>   ADJ   ADV

The simplest and most direct way to expand a sentence is by adding modifiers. While writing that is loaded down with adjectives and adverbs can get boring, we frequently need these modifiers for accuracy and completeness.

For example, the police would want more information than just the following:

> "The man jumped into the car and left the scene."

We might expand this sentence by adding some adjectives and adverbs.

> "The _short, bald_ man jumped into an _old, red_ Ford Mustang and _quickly_
>   ADJ   ADJ   ADV
> left the scene."

Examining How Sentences Work:
Using Prepositional Phrases

A second common way of expanding a sentence is by adding prepositional phrases. A prepositional phrase is always introduced by a preposition. Here are some of the most common prepositions:

at	from	through
by	in	under
down	of	up
for	on	with

Notice how most prepositions bring to the sentence a relation of time and place.
One object is placed **in** another, or **on** another.
One event happened **before** another or **after** another, etc.
A prepositional phrase frequently tells you more about a noun or verb – usually when or where or why.

The doctor *in the emergency room* was told to lie down *in the lounge for a nap*.

Exercise 1: Organizing Basic Sentences to Tell a Story

Below are two lists: a list of nouns and noun phrases and a list of verbs.
Mix and match between the two columns to create as many basic sentences as you can
that string together to develop a single story.

NOUNS AND NOUN PHRASES

seasons
the long
difficult winter
spring
days
students
teachers
baseball games
men and women
gardeners
the school year
summer
vacation
text books
children
holidays
turkeys
houses
no one
everyone
independent
film producers
student
government
representatives

VERBS

change
melts
blossoms
brighten and lengthen
don't study
ease
spring up
mow
plant and weed
ends
passes quickly
close
are distributed and
covered
sulk
approach
are prepared
are decorated
bothers
laughs
budget
meet
worry

What is the main idea of the story you just wrote?

Now, write ten of your own sentences, using your own subjects and verbs. Your sentences should string together to form a discussion of a single idea or a story. Make certain, however, that every sentence has a subject and a verb, or is an imperative (you understood) sentence.

1.

2.

3.

4.

5.

6.

7.

8.

9.

10.

What single idea do your sentences develop? In other words, what is your main idea?

Exercise 2: Composing Mix-and-Match Sentences

The following four lists contain nouns and noun phrases, verbs, indirect objects, and direct objects. Mix and match from among the four lists and compose as many sentences as you can. Be creative. Have fun. Make certain you capitalize the first word of your sentence and use the appropriate ending punctuation.

authors	write	their fans	letters
computer programmers	write	computer	a Christmas
men and women in the military	shoot	code	present
parachute folders	fold	enemy	a pomegranate
tragic heroes	inspire	soldiers	an interview
the girl sitting next to Rhonda	stole	parachutes	autographed
wicked witches	are frightening	readers and	pictures
the judge and jury	convicted	audience	headaches
Mr. and Mrs. Simpson and	rode	members	lunch
their children	sent	Rhonda's	their diamonds
Pablo's aunt in Mexico	gave	algebra notes	tickets
she	offered	small children	
the White House Chief of Staff	send	the defendant	
Hollywood superstars	give	the train	
wild rabbits	bought	him	
the salaried employees	sell	Baki	
South African diamond miners	write	the applicant	
agitated police officers		their fans	
		farmers	
		the secretaries	
		jewelry	
		companies	
		speeders	

Make certain that the adjectives and adverbs that you use to complete the exercise above will add information to the sentence that will help your reader understand the point of the paragraph from which the sentence could have been taken.

Exercise 3: Expanding Sentences with Modifiers

Expand the following sentences by adding modifiers (adjectives and adverbs). Be sure the words you add help the sentence make sense. Try not to use any words more than once.

1. The horse jumped the fence.
The _brown, three-legged_ horse jumped the _broken_ fence.

2. The student threw his book.
The ___frustrated___ student threw his ___dreadful___,
___boring___ book.

3. The woman walked out of the room.
The ___upset___ woman walked ___quickly___ out of the
___sorrow filled___ room.

4. The police officer chased the car.
The ___risky___ police officer ___ferociously___ chased the
___speeding___ car.

5. The soldier picked up his bag and climbed aboard the bus.
The ___new___ soldier ___sadly___ picked up his bag and
___slowly___ climbed aboard the ___green___ bus.

6. The reporter attacked the senator with questions.
The reporter, ___ran___ and ___quickly___, attacked the
___unsuspecting___ senator with ___pressure full___ questions.

7. The boy asked his teacher a question, but a girl in the front seat answered the question.
The ___confused___ boy asked his ___wise___
teacher a question, but a ___perky___ girl in the front seat answered
the ___confusing___ question.

8. The clerk at the register got sick and had to be taken to the hospital.
The clerk at the _____ *cash* _____ register _____ *Suddenly* _____ got
sick and had to be _____ *quickly* _____ taken to the hospital.

9. Jack walked to the back of the store and spoke to the storekeeper.
_____ *Nervous* _____ and _____ *jittery* _____, Jack walked
_____ *confidently* _____ to the back of the store and spoke to the
_____ *cute* _____, storekeeper.

10. The lady got up and gave her seat on the bus to a man.
The _____ *Nice* _____ lady got up and gave her seat on the
_____ *full* _____ bus to a _____ *older* _____ man.

Keep In Mind:

When expanding sentences by adding modifiers like adjectives and adverbs, it is important that you choose your words carefully.

Every word in the sentence (and every sentence in the paragraph) should contribute to the main or overall idea you are developing.

There is no room for irrelevant details—especially if you simply want to make it "look longer," or to meet some word or page count assigned by your teacher. A short but fully developed piece with relevant details is much better than one twice as long, but full of unimportant information.

For example:
In the preceding Exercise 3, sentence 6, if the senator is dishonest, it may not be important to tell the reader that she is young, tall, or friendly.

If sentence 3 is about an angry woman who's walking stormily out of a(n) astonished room, again it may not be important to tell the reader at this time that she is young and tall.

Exercise 4: Expanding Sentences with Prepositional Phrases

Expand each of the following sentences by adding prepositional phrases.

1. I threw the bouquet of flowers to the girl in the back of the room.

2. He bought a soda.

He bought a soda from the boy who sits in the front of the room.

3. She drove her car.

She drove her car into a lake.

4. The soldier aimed his rifle.

The soldier aimed his rifle at the enemy.

5. The woman said hello.

The woman said hello to the man who always feeds the birds in the park.

6. A picture hung there.

A picture hung there during WWII.

7. Mary saw the movie.

Mary saw the movie at her house and was scared.

8. The horse threw him.

The horse threw him from the saddle onto the ground.

9. I passed Joe.

I passed Joe on my bicycle at the park.

10. The boys took a ride.

The boys took a ride on their bikes to the park.

Expand these sentences in the same manner, making sure to include both adjective and adverb modifiers, as well as prepositional phrases.

1. The cowboy <u>from the dude ranch</u> walked <u>at a leisurely pace</u> down the street.

2. A nurse held his hand.

   A nurse from the hospital held his hand during the surgery,

3. A man was hit.

   A man from the store was hit hard by a speeding car.

4. The actor fell.

   The actor in the play fell from the stage,

5. His mother said to leave.

   His mother said to leave immedietly from the show.

Write five original sentences, making sure that each one has at least one prepositional phrase.

1. Drew ran in the park looking for his brother.

2. The razor sharp blade flew from his hand into the target.

3. The ball floated from his hands into mine.

4. The puck launched itself from the ice and hit the top corner,

5. He sprinted across the field yelling for the ball.

Review

Exercise 5: Completing Sentences

Complete these sentences. Try to use concise nouns and adjectives wherever possible.
The first one is done for you as an example.

1. <u>That new yellow car</u> was in an accident.

2. The *uncaught* was arrested in town.
   crook

3. The *old ma*visited their brother. '

4. The *red BMW* turned the corner on two wheels.

5. The *peasant* stole a loaf of bread.

6. The *new churc*caught fire and burned down.

7. The *black cat*climbed the tree and broke a branch.

8. The *young boy* swept and washed the steps.

9. The *football* ran across an open field.
   player

10. The *old* threw a rope to the man on the dock.
    sailor

Complete these sentences by adding a verb and modifiers.

1. The letter on the desk _was sent by his old neighbor._

2. The night football game _was one. by the panthers_

3. The table in the hallway _broke when_ to many peqde sat on it.

4. The desk by the door _had to be_ moved so the door could be opened.

5. A house on the corner _was robbed_ when the family was on vacation.

6. The car across the street _ran into_ a light post to avoid hitting a pedestrian.

7. Our neighbor _got our_ mail for us,

8. Three soldiers on the bus _sang_ . "Yankee Doodle ",

9. A man and his son _ran home_ .

10. On the corner near our house _there was_ a car crash.

The following statements have subjects and verbs, but they are not complete sentences. They need complements to complete the thought. Complete each sentence by adding complements, modifiers, and prepositional phrases.

1. The man hit _a ground ball to center field._

2. The policeman arrested _the criminal who robbed the bank._

3. A nurse at the hospital saw _the gruesome cut on his leg._

4. The story on page one was _a picture of the new mayor._

5. The woman swept _the dirty basement closet._

6. The sailor was _out to sea when the storm hit._

7. Every seventeen years, locusts cause _terrible storms in the sea._

8. A thief is _someone who steals things._

9. For the test she wrote _that the answer to question 6 was A._

10. The judge sentenced _the man to life in prison._

Write five original sentences. Draw lines separating the subject, verb, and complement and label each part in each sentence.
For example:

The view from the deep river gorge │ was │ breathtaking.
      subject   verb   complement
                                     (predicate adjective)

1.

2.

3.

4.

5.

Writing Opportunity: *The Homework Essay: The Précis*

WRITING A PRÉCIS OF A BOOK is very different from writing a book report or review. A précis is a brief discussion of the main point of the work you are studying and how that main point is developed. The précis is, by definition, brief. This presents the greatest challenge—trying to present a full and accurate description of the book or article as concisely as possible.

While *all* of the traits of powerful essays are important in a précis, sentence correctness and completeness probably are most important. Remember, the purpose of the précis is for you to identify the most important ideas of the book, story, or article you have read without wasting words. Since economy counts, you'll want every sentence to carry as much weight as it can.

Remember to use what you have learned about sentence development to create a variety of powerful sentences that clearly establish your focus and help your reader understand your point.

Step 1: *Choose your topic*
What book, story, or article are you going to discuss? You need to include:
- the book's full title,
- the author's full and correct name, and
- the genre (literary type).

Step 2: *Draft the main ideas*
Unlike other forms of writing, your précis focuses on retelling information, not interpreting the information. For this reason, you won't have a thesis *per se,* but you need to know the main ideas of the piece you're discussing. Start by making a list of these main ideas, or key points, in sentence form. For example:

- The plot of *The Dante Club,* by Matthew Pearl, is driven first by a series of gruesome, but apparently unconnected murders throughout Boston in the immediate wake of the Civil War.

- As the friends of beloved poet Ralph Waldo Emerson gather to help him create the first American translation of Dante's *Inferno,* they gradually come to realize that the murders imitate the torments depicted in Dante's Hell.

NOTE: There is very little judgment, interpretation, or evaluation in these sentences. While it might be necessary to offer some conclusions about the work you are discussing, the main purpose of a précis is to retell, not to interpret.

Additionally, since you will not be able to repeat *every* detail from the original in the space allowed (usually a few paragraphs, 100 - 500 words or so, depending on the length of the original), this list of main ideas allows you to narrow your focus to those aspects that are most important.

Time Clue: Assume you have a week to read the article and write your précis. As you read, you should look for the main ideas. Every time you encounter a new main idea in your reading, jot down the idea. Then, when you finish reading, all you need to do is draft the sentences in your own words.

Step 3: *Jot down the key points of development (the details that support the main ideas)*
You do not need a formal outline because your précis will follow the order established by the author of the original.

Reread or skim the book, story, or article you are discussing. Write down the details that support the main ideas that you listed in Step 2.
Remember to follow the order of the original, but to write everything *in your own words.*

Time Clue: Depending on the length of the original, once you have finished reading, you should not need more than an hour or two (for a story or article) or a day or two (for a full-length book) for this step.

Step 4: *Write your first draft*

Turn your list of main ideas and supporting points into paragraphs. This should not be difficult, as you have already identified the main ideas and listed the most important details. This should take only as much time as it takes your hands to physically write or keyboard it.

Time Clue: Less than one day.

Step 5: *Revise and rewrite*

Set your draft aside for at least a day. You need to be able to look at it with fresh eyes in order to revise it effectively. This means that, for a weeklong assignment, you need to build into your schedule a day when you will not even look at the assignment.

Then read it over and look for holes in the information, any places where you could be clearer or more thorough. Have you identified the *most important* points of the original? Are you providing enough of the *most important* details from the original to offer your reader a reasonable sample? Have you considered each and every sentence to make certain that it communicates as clearly and fully as it needs to? You also want to pay attention to grammar, mechanics, spelling, and so on.

Use the scoring rubrics on pages 12, 35, and 45 and make certain your essay demonstrates your mastery.

Show your précis to one or two other people and have them read it and rate it according to the rubrics.

Rewrite the précis, fixing any of the problems you found when you reread it, and those that others found when you asked them to read it.

Finally, create a new, clean draft of the paper.

Time Clue: You have just one day left for this step, but if you've carefully planned and drafted, this is plenty of time.

Step 6: *Turn in your précis*

Trait Four
Conventions of
Written English

TRAIT FOUR:
CONVENTIONS OF WRITTEN ENGLISH

B Y DEFINITION, A CONVENTION is a commonly accepted way of doing things. The adjective *conventional* means "usual" or "traditional." In this book, *convention* simply means the "way it's usually done." Conventions exist for almost every human activity, and writing is no exception; consider, for example, how we usually write from left to right, beginning at the top-left corner of the page.

We readily accept conventions and seldom stray from them because they make our daily lives easier. Imagine how difficult it would be to read books in which the sentences flow from right to left, or top to bottom, when you are accustomed to reading from left to right. Similarly, someone accustomed to reading from top to bottom, which is a convention in some cultures, might have difficulty reading our left-to-right writing.

Beginning every sentence with a capital letter and ending every sentence with some form of end punctuation are also conventions. Read the following paragraph:

> the social movement of feminism found its approach to literature in the 1960s of course, women had already been writing and publishing for centuries, but the 1960s saw the rise of a literary theory that explored the feminine perspective as distinct from the masculine until then, the works of female writers (or works about females) were examined by the same standards as those by male writers (and about men) women were thought to be unintelligent (at least in part because they were generally less formally educated than men), and many women accepted that judgment it was not until the feminist movement was well under way that women began examining old texts to reevaluate their portrayal of women and writing new works to reflect the new consciousness

You can probably figure out what the paragraph says, but without capitalization and punctuation, you need to work harder to understand it than you would if the conventions had been followed.

As the Second Truth says, "Powerful writing is understandable to others," and following conventions is the first step in making your essay understandable.

In this book, you will follow the writing conventions using *Standard Written English*; that is, plain-old "normal" and "usual" English. We will not experiment with dialects as Dickens and Twain do. Nor will we include stream of consciousness like James Joyce and Virginia Woolf.

Another term used for Standard Written English is Standard American Edited English. This simply means that where British English and American English differ in word choice, punctuation, and spelling, this book will follow American English.

We will begin with the most basic elements of writing. Even if the following exercises review things you learned years ago, go ahead and practice them, thinking about how following conventions will help your reader read your writing.

Make Yours Better!

Note that frequent and severe deviations from the Conventions of Written English make this essay extremely difficult to read and understand.

■ Misspellings and the absence of necessary commas render this first paragraph almost meaningless.

■ Incorrect capitalization, improper use of articles, and gross misspellings like "a a parrant" for "an apparent" hinder the reader's ability to identify the writer's point.

■ The absence of quotation marks around the scientist's words creates confusion. Frequent misspellings also make the text difficult to read.

A team of scientists have perdicted the end of life as we know it once again on earth. This time it is a asteroid 1950 DA it scheduled to slam into earth level intire citys and coss massive fires. And tidal waves. And the date of our planetery dance with Density March 16, 2880. A mere 800 years 35 generations away.

Them who thrive on fearmongering point out the vast amounts of energy released by the 1994 colission of Comet shoemaker Levy 9 and the planet Jupiter the 1908 crash of Something from Space in the middle of siberia that destroyed huge areas of woodland. They even like to point to a a parrant earth-metor collision in Mexico. That wiped out the Dinosaurs and lets not forget all of the recent fals allarms most notable the international astronomical unions perdiction in 1998 that in the year 2028 that a "massive asteroid" would smash into the earth that one was dismissed by nasa in less then a day.

Jon Giorgini of NASAs jet proppulsion Labratory who headed the 1950 DA research team explains that its not his goal to insight globle panic. It's so far in the future. It's nothing anyone should worry about, he say adding, But it illustrate the value of understanding things sooner, then, latter. time indeed seem to be the key factor to accurately predict the path of a asteroid. Scientist need to know such things as how the body spins in space.

What it is made of its mass. And how the way it reflects light effects the way it moves in space Such knowledge of 1950 DA does not exist, yet, scientists think it might take years – even decades – to collect the nessary data.

Still the catachysm not scheduled to occur for over 800 years so there plenty of time to study if it is learned that 1950 DA pose a serious threat the hundred's of years' warning give us ample time to devise a way to defect or destroy it.

So you can take off. you're hard hat. And stop digging your underground shelter. The earth is safe. As safe as it ever was.

Essay Critique

This essay is riddled with spelling and punctuation errors, as well as several errors in noun case and subject-verb agreement. Furthermore, there are several sentences in which the verb is missing altogether. If these errors were fixed, the essay would be interesting, informative, and fairly well organized.

This essay receives a score of ❶ on the:

Conventions Rubric

5 = Essay is largely free of basic surface errors. Errors that do appear (semi-colon, complex subject-verb agreement, etc.) suggest an attempt to experiment with more sophisticated language and may interfere with the reader's understanding, requiring extensive revision.

4 = DEVELOPING
Essay is largely free of basic surface errors (spelling, elementary punctuation, capitalization, etc.), but correctness of language is largely governed by simplicity of language.

3 = Surface errors may be frequent but do not severely interfere with the reader's understanding of the essay. Correctness of language is largely governed by simplicity of language.

2 = Basic surface errors (spelling, elementary punctuation, capitalization, etc.) are frequent and varied enough to indicate a lack of understanding of the fundamentals of standard written English. Frequency and variety of errors interfere with the reader's understanding.

❶ = NOVICE
Surface errors may be frequent and extreme, and severely interfere with the reader's understanding of the essay. Correctness of language is largely governed by simplicity of language.

Part I: Basic Punctuation

- Begin *every* standard written English sentence with a capital letter.
- End every standard written English sentence with an appropriate end-punctuation mark (. ? !).

Exercise 1: Using Capitalization and Punctuation Correctly

Correct each of the following sentences by capitalizing the first word and inserting the correct end punctuation mark. Then, explain why you chose the end punctuation mark that you did.

Incorrect: how many years does it take for an oak tree to reach maturity

Correction: How many years does it take for an oak tree to reach maturity?

Explanation: I used the question mark at the end because the first word of the sentence, "how," clearly introduces a question.

1. nathaniel Hawthorne was born in Salem, Massachusetts

Correction: Nathaniel Hawthorne was born in Salem, Massachusetts,

Explanation: Nathaniel is a name and their needs to be a Period at the end of the sentence.

2. his ancestors were wealthy, influential people

Correction: His ancestors were wealthy, influential people.

Explanation: His is the beginning of the sentence and there needs to be a period at the end of the sentence,

3. one, William Hathorne, became a judge who persecuted Quakers

Correction: One, William Hathorne, became a judge who persecuted Quakers.

Explanation: One is at the beginning of the sentence and there needs to be a period at the end of the sentence.

4. another, John Hathorne, sentenced many Salem women to death for witchcraft

Correction: Another, John Hathorne, sentenced many Salem to death for witchcraft.

Explanation: Another is the beginning of the sentence and there needs to be a period at the end.

5. how horrible it must have been for young Hawthorne to know about these notorious men in his own family

Correction: How horrible it must have been for young Hawthorne to know about these notorious men in his own family.

Explanation: How is at the beginning of the sentence and there needs to be a period at the end.

6. is it any wonder that Hawthorne changed his name—however slightly—by adding the "w" at the end of the first syllable

Correction: Is it any wonder that Hawthorne changed his name—however slightly—by adding the "w" at the end of the first syllable?

Explanation: Is is at the beginning of sentence and there needs to be a question mark at the end.

Commas

Inside a sentence, use commas to:

- separate items in a series of three or more

Billy, Rosalinda, and Tyrone went to the diner and bought hamburgers, fries, and diet sodas.
(Note that there *is* a comma before the "and" in the list of three or more.)

- separate the noun being addressed directly from the rest of the sentence.

And you, my friend, are the one person I know I can trust.
Sally, would you please close the door?
And this concludes our tour, ladies and gentlemen.

- separate nonessential information (that which does not change the meaning of the main idea) from the main part of the sentence.

My mother, who has won several art awards, *was appointed chairperson of the decorating committee.*
Chantal accepted her diploma from the principal, who mispronounced her name.
My all-time favorite book, A Tale of Two Cities, *has been dramatized many times in stage plays, movies, and television shows.*
(Note: do *not* use commas to set off information that *does* change the meaning of the main idea: *The athletes who participated in fall sports were given special consideration on their mid-term exams.*)

- indicate the end of a subordinate clause that introduces the sentence.

After all was said and done, it was a good party.
Since no one came who had not been invited, there was no damage to Romero's house.
Once the party was over, we all helped Romero clean his house.

- indicate the end of a prepositional, adjectival, or adverbial phrase that introduces the sentence.

By tomorrow, I hope to have my paper finished.

After the prom, many students go out to breakfast at a local diner.

Approximately every eighty years, Halley's Comet appears in the skies over Earth.

- separate the clauses in a compound sentence.

The rain came down, and the floods came up.

The Greeks may have invented geometry, but algebra was developed in Arabia.

You can wear the clothes I laid out for you, or you can stay home.

(Note: place the comma before the coordinating conjunction.)

Exercise 2: Using Commas Correctly

Place commas where they belong in the following sentences and then explain why you have placed commas where you have. If there are any sentences in which you do not place commas, explain why.

Incorrect: While Marietta was taking her exam the teacher who had accused her of cheating watched her like a hawk.

Correction: While Marietta was taking her exam, the teacher who had accused her of cheating watched her like a hawk.

Explanation: I placed a comma after "exam" because that was the end of the introductory subordinate clause. I did not place a comma before "who" because that clause contains more than "extra" information. It actually specifies which teacher watched her.

1. When Hawthorne was four his father died, and this resulted in a series of unfortunate circumstances that created a lonely childhood for the boy.

   Correction: When H...

   Explanation: It is a comma fanboy because your setting off the subordinate clause.

2. In 1837, he published *Twice Told Tales* and earned great national fame.

   Correction:

   Explanation: Introductory prepositional phrase because there...

3. His stories won the admiration of Edgar Allan Poe, who considered Hawthorne a genius.

Correction:

Explanation: It is a subordinate clause after the comma.

4. Another contemporary of Hawthorne, Herman Melville, who wrote *Moby Dick*, became Hawthorne's close friend.

Correction:

Explanation: To designate a subordinate clause.

5. During his life, Hawthorne was friendly with Transcendentalists, Ralph Waldo Emerson and Henry David Thoreau.

Correction:

Explanation: Introductary prepositional phrase.

6. "Young Goodman Brown," "Dr. Heidigger's Experiment," and "The Celestial Railroad" are among Hawthorne's best-known stories.

Correction:

Explanation: Seperating three objects

Commas Really Make a Difference

Pablo invited his friends, Alex, and Anna to his birthday party.

Pablo invited his friends, Alex and Anna, to his birthday party.

Dashes

Inside a sentence, use dashes to:

- set off major shifts in topic or tone.

> *William Shakespeare and George Bernard Shaw—each considered a genius in his own lifetime—are often taught together in the same course.*
>
> *It really did not seem clear to Jaqueline—although you tried several times to explain it—why her clothing was not appropriate for a job interview.*

- introduce an informal list.

> *Such courses cover many topics—the evolution of comic drama, the impact of technology on the theatre, and the status of the playwright in his society.*
>
> *There are many reasons—lack of money and lack of time among them—why I cannot go.*

Exercise 3: Using Commas and Dashes Correctly

Place commas and/or dashes where they belong in the following sentences and then explain why you have placed them where you have. If there are any sentences in which you do not place commas or dashes, explain the reason why.

Incorrect:	The house was beautiful, but the location directly across the river from a nuclear power plant was less than perfect.
Correction:	*The house was beautiful, but the location—directly across the river from a nuclear power plant—was less than perfect.*
Explanation:	*I set off the phrase, "directly across the river from a nuclear power plant," with dashes because it was additional information, but a fairly big shift in topic from the main idea of the sentence. Commas would also have worked, but the dashes emphasize the shift more.*

1. One of the most far-reaching pieces of legislation of the entire nineteenth century was the 1834 Poor Law Amendment Act also known as the "New Poor Law" which abolished systems of poor relief that had existed since the passing of the Elizabethan Poor Law of 1601.

Correction:

Explanation:

2. While the old poor law had established "parishes" throughout Britain each responsible for assisting its own poor this New Poor Law combined parishes into unions to administer assistance to the poor.

Correction:

Explanation:

3. Every union maintained a workhouse that housed people who were unable to support themselves.

Correction:

Explanation:

4. If people sent to the workhouse were found to be fit they were put to work.

Correction:

Explanation:

5. Giving money food and clothing to the poor in their own community was deemed too expensive especially as the number of unemployed increased every day.

Correction:

Explanation:

6. People confined to a workhouse even the children would have letters sewn onto their clothing "P" for pauper followed by the letter of the parish.

Correction:

Explanation:

Part II: Basic Grammar: Subject-Verb Agreement

Be aware of the exact subject of the sentence.

- Simple, one-word subjects and one-word verbs are easy to identify.

    <u>Michael</u> <u>throws</u> the ball.
        s   *v*

    <u>Cynthia</u> <u>runs</u> down the street.
        s   *v*

- Sometimes the subject is part of a longer phrase or is followed by a long phrase or clause that might make the simple subject less clear.

    The clear, blue autumn <u>sky</u> <u>is</u> a lovely sight.
                  s *v*

    The last <u>time</u> I saw the sunrise <u>was</u> last summer.
          s   *v*

Exercise 4: Identifying the Simple Subject

Underline the simple subject in each of the following sentences. Then, explain why you think the word you have selected is the simple subject.

For example:
The <u>people</u> in the market district of the city were affected by the blackout.

Explanation: *"People" is the simple subject because it is the people who were affected by the blackout, not the market district or the city.*

1. As a literary criticism theory, the Formalist <u>approach</u> to literature was developed at the beginning of the 20th century.

Explanation: It is what the story is about

2. Today, <u>formalism</u> is generally regarded as a stuffy, rigid, and inaccessible means to read literature.

Explanation: It is what the story is reffering to.

3. Like classical artists such as da Vinci and Michaelangelo, <u>Formalists</u> concentrate more on the form of the art rather than the content.

Explanation: The story is reffering to it.

4. This <u>theory</u>, unlike most other popular approaches to literature, demands no study or research beyond the text itself.

Explanation: It is what they are talking about.

5. An <u>approach</u> such as this makes classical literature more accessible to all levels of readers.

Explanation: Describing this word in the story

- Sometimes the subject is actually a verb form acting like a noun.

- Infinitives are sometimes used like nouns in sentences.

> <u>To run</u> for President sounds like a lot of work.
>
> <u>To represent</u> the constituents of the ninety-second Congressional District is the job of whomever we elect.

- Present participles can be used like nouns in sentences. These are called gerunds.

> <u>Running</u> and <u>swimming</u> are both excellent aerobic activities.
>
> <u>Building</u> that new house of hers is the only thing Ariadne can talk about these days.

- Sometimes the subject is actually a phrase or clause.

> <u>That you forgot</u> is no excuse.
>
> <u>Why you can't follow the simplest instructions</u> is a mystery to me.
>
> <u>Where you go</u> and <u>what you do</u> are of no concern to me.

Exercise 5: Identifying the Complete Subject

Underline the subject in each of the following sentences. Remember that the subject might be a verb form or a phrase or clause acting like a noun. Then, explain why you think the word, phrase, or clause you have selected is the subject.

For example:
<u>To live and let live</u> is often a difficult philosophy to live by.

Explanation: The entire phrase "to live and let live" is the subject because the entire phrase explains the "philosophy" talked about in the predicate of the sentence.

1. Compulsive exercising will not lead to better health.

Explanation:

2. To get better grades was the reason Hiram hired a tutor.

Explanation:

3. Reading and writing are two of the most important skills taught in school.

Explanation:

4. Half-past ten was Dominic's curfew.

Explanation:

5. "Here, Kitty, Kitty," is the punch line to the joke about the 100-pound parrot.

Explanation:

- The subject is not always at the beginning of the sentence.

> *Until you have finished your homework, <u>watching</u> television is out of the question.*
>
> *There are no <u>excuses</u> for your rude behavior.*
>
> *Until now, didn't the <u>benefits</u> of exercise ever occur to you?*

Exercise 6: Finding the Simple Subject

Underline the simple subject in each of the following sentences. Remember that the actual subject might not come at the beginning of the sentence. In the space provided, explain why you think the word you have selected is the simple subject.

For example:
Without a doubt, <u>Sam</u> read the most books last summer.

Explanation: *Although "doubt" is a noun that comes early in the sentence, "doubt" has not read the books—Sam has, so Sam is the simple subject.*

1. For all intents and purposes, the quality of one's life is determined by the nature of his or her friends.

   Explanation:

2. Instead of running, vigorous walking seems to be the favored exercise of older adults.

   Explanation:

3. Because of her extra effort last marking period, Laraketa made the honor roll.

   Explanation:

4. Throughout the lush, green meadow, delicate young deer stood grazing in the early morning hours.

Explanation:

5. Located far north of the city, the small village relied heavily on farming proceeds.

Explanation:

NOTE: The following conventions are true of every subject regardless of where the subject is placed in the sentence, and regardless of whether the subject is one word, a phrase, a clause, or a verb form acting as a noun. Although you are accustomed to finding the subject before the verb, in inverted sentences, you will find the *verb* before the *subject*.

- Number (singular or plural) The number of the simple subject determines the number of the verb.

> *That person (singular) is (singular) the one I was talking about.*
>
> *Those people (plural) are (plural) the ones I was talking about.*
>
> *Despite the delay because of the weather, there were (plural) several people (plural) waiting to see the kickoff.*

- No matter how many nouns might be in the complete subject of the sentence, it is only the *simple subject* that affects the verb.

> *The Martians (plural), who planned their invasion of earth for over a year, were (plural) ultimately defeated by a simple virus.*
>
> *The cold virus (singular), probably the most common and virulent of all viruses, causes (singular) more deaths each year than people realize.*

- When connected with the conjunction "and," a compound subject (subject with two or more *simple subjects*) is almost always treated like a plural subject and will take a plural verb.

<u>Bonita</u> and <u>Marcos</u> (compound subject) **are** (plural) *planning their own anniversary party.*

Not to be forgotten as the fundamentals of a good education **are** (plural) <u>reading, writing,</u> and basic <u>arithmetic</u> (compound subject).

- When the compound subject uses the conjunctions "or," "nor," "either...or," or "neither...nor" to connect a singular and a plural component, it is better practice to place the plural word(s) of the subject closest to the verb and use a plural verb. Otherwise, the verb must agree in number with the closest subject.

<u>Andrew</u> *or his* <u>sisters</u> <u>are</u> *in charge of invitations and decorations.*

The compound subject is joined by "or"; the subject closest to the verb is plural, so the verb is plural.

There <u>is</u> *either an* <u>apple</u> *or some* <u>berries</u> *in the refrigerator.*

The compound subject is joined by "either...or"; the subject closest to the verb is singular, so the verb is singular.

Neither the hockey <u>players</u> *nor their* <u>coach</u> <u>knows</u> *the reason for the ice*

The compound subject is joined by "neither...nor"; the subject closest to the verb is singular, so the verb is singular.

rink's closure.

Exercise 7: Making Subjects and Verbs Agree

Underline the simple subject(s) in each of the following sentences and circle the correct form of the verb. Then, explain why you think the words you have selected are the subjects.

For example:

Nora's <u>opinion</u>, formed without the least regard for anyone else's feelings, [(was) | were] that only she should receive the treat.

Explanation: *"Opinion" is the simple subject, as the verb links "opinion" and the predicate nominative. Since "opinion" is a singular noun, the verb must also be singular.*

1. Mary and Harry [**is** | **are**] going to the beach.

Explanation:

2. Despite the rain, the possibilities for travel [**is** | **are**] countless.

Explanation:

3. Limiting the amount of time the students can work on the computers [**is** | **are**] not a good idea.

Explanation:

4. The enjoyment of our clients and their well-being [**is** | **are**] our primary goal(s).

Explanation:

5. All of the books except this one [**was** | **were**] published by Hillyard, Inc.

Explanation:

6. Performing difficult dance steps in front of a live audience [**takes** | **take**] a lot of courage.

Explanation:

7. In the fog, either a lighthouse or several extremely bright lights [**warns** | **warn**] ships of the cape's shallow waters.

Explanation:

8. Screaming rude comments and stomping your feet [**is** | **are**] not appropriate ways to acknowledge the performers.

Explanation:

9. The players on the women's soccer team [**practices** | **practice**] diligently to prepare for the state championship.

Explanation:

10. Either Mr. Dratch or the members of the stage crew [**prepares** | **prepare**] the set and costumes for the musical.

Explanation:

Part II: Basic Grammar: Pronoun—Antecedent Clarity

Make it perfectly clear to whom or what all of your pronouns refer.

- The antecedent must appear in the text *before* the pronoun to which it refers, either in the preceding sentence or earlier in the same sentence.

> The **professor** was pleased to hear **he** had been awarded the grant.
>
> At the reception, the speaker announced that the **professor** had won the grant. When **he** heard **his** name, **he** stood and accepted the audience's applause.

- Each pronoun must refer to a specific antecedent.

Incorrect: *The professor told the graduate student that **he** had won an award.* (Has the professor or the graduate student won the award?)

Better: *The **professor** mentioned the award **he** had won to the graduate student.* (Here it is clear that the professor won the award.)

*The professor congratulated the graduate **student** on the award **he** had won.* (Here it is clear that the graduate student has won the award.)

Pronouns Tell Us Who It Is

The doctor told Buford that he needed complete bed rest.

Exercise 8: Making Pronouns and Antecedents Agree

Rewrite each of the following sentences to clarify which of the nouns is the proper antecedent for each pronoun.

Incorrect:	Kay and Jane saw the children in the orphanage and thought that they were the luckiest people in the world.
Correction:	Kay and Jane thought they were the luckiest people in the world after they saw the children in the orphanage.
Explanation:	It is unlikely that Kay and Jane thought the orphans were the luckiest people alive, so the sentence must reflect that "Kay and Jane" are the compound antecedent of the pronoun "they." Reordering the sentence so that the pronoun appears after "Kay and Jane" but before "the children" clarifies the confusion.

1. When Leandra told Marissa about her interview, she was so excited that she cried.

    Correction:

    Explanation:

2. The managers told the warehouse workers that they would all have to work harder to keep their jobs.

    Correction:

    Explanation:

3. John told Alexander that he needed to go to visit his mother in the nursing home.

Correction:

Explanation:

4. Shawn tried to teach his brother to drive, but he had an accident.

Correction:

Explanation:

5. Lexi promised to give Michonne a copy of her favorite poem.

Correction:

Explanation:

Part II: Basic Grammar: Pronoun—Antecedent Agreement

Like nouns, pronouns express number (singular and plural). The antecedent determines the number of the pronoun. The pronoun and the antecedent *must* agree in number and gender.

- The distributive pronouns, "each," "either" and "neither," are *singular* and refer only to *singular* antecedents.

- "None" is *singular* and must refer to a *singular* noun.

- Pairs or lists of nouns connected by "and" are treated like *plural* nouns. The agreeing pronouns must also be *plural*.

- Singular collectives, like "group," "family," "flock," etc. are usually treated like *singular* nouns with very few exceptions. A pronoun referring to a collective noun must also be *singular*.

- Singular nouns that are not gender specific (doctor, student, person, etc.) are *singular* and properly followed by a *singular* pronoun. It is the writer's choice which gender pronoun to use (he or she, him or her, she/he, him/her).

- Pronouns must also agree in gender with gender-specific nouns (man ... he/him; princess ... she/her, etc.)

Make Sure Your Pronouns Match Their Antecedents!

One of the ladies wore their hats to church.

Exercise 9: Choosing the Correct Pronoun

Fill in the blanks in the following sentences with the correct pronoun. Then, write a brief explanation of why you chose the pronoun that you did.

For example:
Each of the women packed her lunch for the journey.

Explanation: The pronoun in the blank refers to the word "each," which is singular. The prepositional phrase "of the women" tells us that we need to use a feminine pronoun. "Her" is the feminine, singular pronoun that best completes the sentence.

1. If you see Vinnie and Ramona, please tell _____ that I will be at _____ party.

Explanation:

2. Neither Joanna nor La Shonda remembered to bring _____ toothbrush.

Explanation:

3. The entire team celebrated _____ coach's birthday by dumping a cooler of ice on _____.

Explanation:

4. When either Brandi or Shelia arrives, please ask _____ to wait in the living room.

Explanation:

5. The student who wants to do well on _____ exam should study.

   Explanation:

6. Whenever either Jason or Pablo asks me to do something, _____ always treats me like a menial servant.

   Explanation:

7. The principal asked every student to bring _____ own lunch to school on the days when the cafeteria is being remodeled.

   Explanation:

8. One of the doctors left _____ stethoscope in the nurse's office after giving physicals for the sports teams.

   Explanation:

9. George's great-aunt Bernadette vowed to leave _____ entire fortune to George and his sisters.

   Explanation:

10. Some time next week, our geometry teacher will surprise _____ with a pop quiz.

   Explanation:

Review

Exercise 10: Following the Conventions of Capitalization

Correct the capitalization in the following sentences.

1. she went to the store for julie to get the new york times.

2. Sarah wanted to go on the Class Trip to New York in June, but she had to pass Chemistry first.

3. My Mother said, "Stop biting your nails."

4. The Hotel he went to was called Akely Towers.

5. to get to bay view, you must drive north on route 369.

6. He lived in the White House at the Corner of Sixteenth Street and Twelfth Avenue.

7. The President of the Senior Class got Straight A's.

8. "You may want to go to Penn State, but I want you to go to your Father's College," Mother said.

9. I know that my Dental appointment is this Summer, but I can't remember if it is with Dr. Harper or Dr. Quinn.

10. Keith, Larry, Jerry, Doug, Jason, and Jim all took the Train to the Stadium to see The New York Yankees play The Boston Red Sox.

11. Chrissy, Emily, Jaimie, and Elizabeth went to the Theater to see the New Play by Tom Stoppard.

12. I was Born in Detroit, Michigan; but I grew up in Cleveland, Ohio.

13. did you live in the south before you moved to new jersey?

14. The Dog, a Siberian Husky, was pure white, so Sasha named him Snowstorm.

15. My Favorite Story as a Child was *Winnie-The-Pooh,* but I also liked *Bambi.*

16. When you were in Italy last Spring, did you go North to see the Leaning Tower of Pisa?

17. The Dentist said, "Open your mouth."

18. Sondra thought it would be funny to do her Math homework in French.

19. Go South on Washington Highway and then make a Left at Crosley Street.

20. I like to visit the Homes of Famous People when I go to Hollywood.

Exercise 11: Making Subjects and Verbs Agree

Select the form of the verb in each sentence that agrees with the subject.

1. Two boys from school [**was** | **were**] missing from homeroom the next morning.

2. One of the books [**has** | **have**] incorrect information.

3. Silently, the girls hiding in the closet [**creeps** | **creep**] from the darkened room.

4. The frightened scout furiously [**attacks** | **attack**] the snake with a stick.

5. [**Was** | **Were**] there enough potato chips for everyone?

6. Where [**is** | **are**] the herd of elephants going?

7. [Was | **Were**] the police officers frightened?

8. Each member of the committee [**is** | are] expected to cast a vote.

9. All members of the club [is | **are**] ready to face the challenge.

10. Either Mona or I [**am** | are] going to have to get up earlier in the morning.

11. Jim and his teammates [is | **are**] playing above their heads.

12. Brian and his friend [**miss** | misses] most of what she says.

13. Either Bianca or one of her friends [**is** | are] going to host the party.

14. Neither the farmers nor the real estate developer [is | **are**] going to give in.

15. Both executives [has | **have**] decided to go to the conference.

16. [**Was** | Were] the executive board willing to pay for transportation?

17. The board of city managers [**is** | are] planning to meet on the third Thursday of every month.

18. The chairpersons of every subcommittee [is | **are**] then going to discuss the outcome of the meeting.

19. There [**is** | are] a mosque, a synagogue, and a chapel on Churchill Street between Ninth and Tenth Avenues.

20. The United Nations [is | **are**] meeting to find a solution to the current world crisis.

Exercise 12: Using Commas Correctly

Insert commas where they belong in the following sentences.

1. The shopkeeper said he'd sell me the food, only if I gave him cold hard cash.

2. I wanted to pay him, but I had only my checkbook and a credit card.

3. Morton, do you have any idea how embarrassing it is to have to return all that merchandise back to the shelves?

4. The salt, pepper, bread, oregano, and parmesan cheese all had to be returned.

5. Samuel, the grumpy shopkeeper, would not help me.

6. While I returned each piece to its shelf, he just watched and sneered.

7. I highly doubt I will ever shop there, again.

8. Imagine Morton, he'd take only cash no check or credit card or even a debit card.

9. That's not a good way to do business, my friend.

10. Now, Herman, the man who owns the little grocery store on the corner is a very nice man.

11. Not only is he flexible in the types of payment, he will accept, he'll have one of his assistants deliver your groceries for you.

12. When I was laid up with my broken leg, that came in very handy.

13. You remember my broken leg, don't you?

14. I fell while looking at the Christmas lights, in Mannheim, Pennsylvania.

15. For a small town, Mannheim has one of the most beautiful light displays I've seen.

16. It reminds me of *It's a Wonderful Life,*an excellent old film.

17. In that movie/ which appears on television almost every year, the main character meets his guardian angel.

18. This character George Bailey, played by Jimmy Stewart, is discouraged and the angel comes to help him.

19. Donna Reed plays his wife and she is one of my favorite actresses.

20. I do like a good old Christmas movie don't you Morton?

Writing Opportunity: *The Homework Essay: The Assigned Topic Essay*

PRACTICALLY EVERY CLASS you take, especially in college, will require you to write essays because the essay is one of the best ways for your teacher to assess what you really know. (Multiple choice, matching, and true-false tests allow the lucky guesser to pretend he or she knows something he or she doesn't really know.)

The essay also allows *you*, the student, to emphasize your strengths and play down your weaknesses. A skillful writer can slant the written piece in any chosen direction. In a writing assignment, *you* are much more in control than on a typical, objective test.

Do not make the mistake that many unfortunate students make and assume that writing skill doesn't "count" on essays written for classes other than English. If you cannot communicate what you know clearly and effectively, your teacher will not be able to make an accurate assessment of how well you know the material.

Because you don't want poor language usage to hide the fact that you do know the subject matter, grammar and mechanics become especially important in non-English-class essays.

Step 1: *Choose an authentic topic*
On a homework essay, the topic will probably be assigned to you. At best, you might be given a list of possible topics from which to choose.

Step 2: *Develop your thesis*

Remember that good writing is the result of good thinking. If you can't explain your point in one sentence, you probably don't understand the point yourself. And it is in the development of your thesis that you take control of your topic, especially an assigned topic.

Since you will probably not be able to exhaust your topic in the space and time allowed (usually a few days and a few pages), your thesis is your opportunity to narrow your topic down to the points you understand the most.

For example:

Let's say you're assigned to write an essay on the contributions of Dr. Seuss to children's literature. There is much you do not know about this topic, but you do understand how Dr. Seuss's wordplay made reading fun and motivated a lot of young children to read and enjoy being read to.

This is the aspect of the topic you will focus on in your thesis.

> While the name Theodore Geisel may not be familiar to many people, no one can question how his alter-ego, beloved children's writer Dr. Seuss, turned a whole generation of pre-school-aged children onto reading through his brilliant use of rhythm, rhyme, onomatopoeia, pun, and other forms of wordplay.

Notice how the writer has actually specified the types of wordplay in the thesis. This will help to keep on topic in later steps.

Step 3: *Freewrite your essay*

Since you've already been able to identify rhythm, rhyme, onomatopoeia, and pun, this should not be a difficult step. Now, you write a very rough draft explaining your thesis.

Time Clue: Let's assume you've been given one week for this essay (the assignment was made on Monday, and the essay is due Friday). You should complete your thesis and freewriting on Monday.

Remember that this step is little more than brainstorming. Never presume that this "draft" will ever be what you submit.

Step 4: *Develop your support*

You cannot discuss Dr. Seuss's use of rhyme without actually offering examples (direct quotations) from his stories and poems. The same holds true of your discussion of his use of rhyme, onomatopoeia, and pun.

> **NOTE:** this is the step where you decide that—if you cannot find enough (three to five for an average essay) examples of a particular device—you should eliminate that item from your thesis and do not promise to discuss it.

By the same token, if you find several examples of a device not mentioned in your thesis, add it to both your thesis and your discussion, if space permits.

Step 5: *Organize*

Think like your intended reader. What is a logical order in which to discuss your ideas? Are there any concepts that need to be understood *before* others can be appreciated? Are there any ideas that need to be introduced and defined *before* you can discuss the concepts of your paper?

Which concepts are key ideas, and which are supporting details?

Choose the style of organization that works best for you to show the relationships among all of your ideas. You may want to use a traditional outline, a word web, or something else.

Step 6: *Gather more support*

> **Time Clue:** If you're going to have a good final draft to turn in Friday, you'll want to complete Steps 4–6 on Tuesday.

Compare your outline with your freewrite and read, research, or brainstorm to fill in any holes in your information.

Step 7: *Write your real first draft*

Again, make it as good as you can. This is not the same freewrite you did before.

Time Clue: Write your first draft on Wednesday.

Step 8: *Revise and rewrite*

Set your draft aside for a day or so. Then pick it up and read it fresh.

Read it as if you are your own audience.
- Is all of the information you want to present there?
- Is it written in the clearest language? Is it in the most logical order?
- Are your grammar, mechanics, spelling, and other uses of language correct?

Use the scoring rubrics on pages 12, 35, 54, and 78 and make certain your essay demonstrates your mastery.

Show your draft to one or two other people and have them read it and rate it according to the rubrics.

Rewrite the essay, fixing any of the problems you found when you reread it, and those that others found when you asked them to read it

Time Clue: All revision and rewriting is done Thursday.

Step 9: *Your essay is finished. Submit it.*

Applying
the
Third Truth

Powerful writing is painless to read.

3
Simple Truths
and
6
Essential Traits
of

Powerful Writing

fatal see FATE

Fade see EASY

Facsimile see COPY 2.

Factor see COMPONENT

Fad see CRAZE

Fade see DIM

Fan see ENTHUSIAST

Faint see WEAK

Fair 1. Fair, unbiased, just, impartial, equitable: free from suspicion or favoritism for any particular side of an issue

FAIR is characterized by frankness, honesty, and an absence of prejudice—said of persons, character, or conduct; as, a fair man; fair dealing, a fair statement. "I would call it *fair* play." —William Shakespeare. *ant.* unfair, dishonest, prejudiced

UNBIASED is characterized by the absolute absence of prejudice in considering a situation. "The lawyers search for *unbiased* jurors." *ant.* biased, partial, partisan

JUST indicates a sense of righteousness, decency, and virtue when acting and making decisions. "The parties awaited a *just* resolution from the arbitrator." *ant.* unjust, unfair, undeserved

IMPARTIAL indicates complete fairness and an absence of favoritism for any party in making a decision. "Our justice system ensures that the judge will be *impartial* when deciding the sentence." *ant.* partial, prejudiced, one-sided

EQUITABLE stresses fairness and equal treatment. "Our Constitution emphasizes *equitable* treatment of all citizens under the law." *ant.* inequitable, undue, unfair, unbalanced

Trait Five
Word Choice

TRAIT FIVE:
WORD CHOICE

MANY NOVICE WRITERS think that "good writing" is about using "fancy-sounding language." Ironically, in their attempts to sound "fancy," these writers make their writing less powerful than it could be.

As with all of the other traits of powerful essays, word choice is fundamental to helping the reader understand the essay. As a writer, your goal is to make your writing clear and interesting, *not* to try to impress your reader with forced cleverness or affected intelligence achieved through "big words."

As with the other traits, powerful word choice is a matter of planning and practice. It should go without saying that you must first know what you are going to say before you attempt to say it. Think and plan before you speak.

Make Yours Better!

Note that poor Word Choice ruins the effectiveness of this otherwise decent essay.

You like the colors as leaves change color in the fall. But did you ever wonder why this happens?

Leaves make the plants' food. Plants take water from the ground through their roots. They take a gas from the air. Plants use sunlight to make a kind of sugar. Plants use sugar as food and for growing. A chemical that gives plants their green color is what allows plants to use sunlight to make sugar from water and gas.

As summer ends and it becomes fall, the days get shorter.

During winter, there is not enough sunlight or water for plants to make food. So they begin to shut down their food factories. The green disappears from the leaves. As the green disappears, you begin to see yellow and orange colors. These colors have been in the leaves all along, but we can't see them in the summer, because they are covered up by the green.

The reds and purples are made mostly in the fall. In some trees, sugar is stuck in the leaves after the food-making stops. Sunlight and the cool nights of fall turn this sugar a red color. The brown color of leaves is made from bad stuff left in the leaves.

It is the combination of all these things that make the colors we like in the fall.

- The vague and simple diction in this essay is more appropriate for a third grade audience than ninth grade.
- The essay lacks necessary factual, scientific terminology.
- It would also be helpful to introduce the term "photosynthesis."
- Repetition is a problem. Varied word choice would make the essay easier to read and understand.
- Red and brown are colors; therefore, it is redundant to say "a red color," and "a brown color."
- What is this "bad stuff" left in the leaves that makes them brown?

Essay Critique

The word choice in this essay is so vague and repetitive that the facts of the issue are not adequately communicated.

This essay receives a score of 1 on the:

Word Choice Rubric

5 = Word choice shows strong attempts at vividness, but vague and inexact language predominates. Figurative language (similes, metaphors, allusions) is unoriginal, and does not really contribute to the overall effect of the essay.

4 = DEVELOPING
Attempts at vividness are more frequent and intentional, but miss the mark, often resulting in clichés, awkward constructions, and an overuse of adjective-noun and adverb-verb phrases, especially overuse of amplifiers like "very," "truly," etc.

3 = Infrequent and tentative attempts at vividness result in clichés and awkward constructions.

2 = Word choice is vague, simplistic, and repetitive. There is no real attempt to use figurative language for clearer, more effective communication.

1 = NOVICE
Word choice is inexact and vague, largely affected by the writer's limited vocabulary. There is no real attempt to use figurative language for clearer, more effective communication.

How *(really)* to Use a Thesaurus

While the thesaurus can be a very powerful tool for a writer, it can also be a careless writer's downfall. Not all synonyms possess identical definitions and connotations, and if you simply replace what you consider a "common" word with a "fancier-sounding" word you found in the thesaurus, you will, quite possibly, use the new word incorrectly and end up sounding foolish.

For example, the listing of synonyms of "popular" in many thesauri includes the word "vulgar" in that "popular" essentially means "of the people," and "vulgar" carries the meaning of "belonging to the common people, the masses." Yet, we commonly use "popular" to mean "well-liked" and "vulgar" to mean "crass or crude."

Therefore, if you've written the sentence, "Jimmy Fallon is a *popular* comedian," and decide to substitute "vulgar" for "popular" (because you checked the thesaurus and it "sounds fancier"), your sentence becomes, "Jimmy Fallon is a *vulgar* comedian," which is not what you want to say at all.

In short, you need to know what the synonym in the thesaurus means and how it is used before you can safely and effectively adopt it in your own writing.

Exercise 1: Finding the Right Word

You will need a thesaurus and a dictionary to complete this exercise.

- *Use a thesaurus and find three synonyms for each target word below.*

- *Look up each of the synonyms in a dictionary.*

- *Write a sentence using each synonym, <u>making certain that each sentence reflects what is unique about the synonym's dictionary definition.</u>*

- *After each sentence, write a brief explanation of why you chose to use that synonym in that way.*

For example:

FIRE: flame   conflagration   inferno

Sentence 1: The draft from the window was so strong it extinguished the candle's flame.

Explanation: Flame is the "gaseous part" of the fire. A huge fire may be made up of several flames. The word does not carry with it the same violent associations as the other synonyms do.

Sentence 2: Entire neighborhoods were destroyed in the conflagration known as the Great Chicago Fire.

Explanation: Conflagration is defined as a large, destructive fire.

Sentence 3: Aileen's priceless record collection was reduced to blobs of black vinyl in the inferno.

Explanation: The definition of inferno highlights the intense heat.

1. TALK: _____   _____   _____

Sentence 1:

Explanation:

Sentence 2:

Explanation:

Sentence 3:

Explanation:

2. THRIFTY: _____   _____   _____

Sentence 1:

Explanation:

Sentence 2:

Explanation:

Sentence 3:

Explanation:

3. WALK: _____   _____   _____

Sentence 1:

Explanation:

Sentence 2:

Explanation:

Sentence 3:

Explanation:

4 LOUD: _____ _____ _____

Sentence 1:

Explanation:

Sentence 2:

Explanation:

Sentence 3:

Explanation:

5. PRETTY: _____ _____ _____

Sentence 1:

Explanation:

Sentence 2:

Explanation:

Sentence 3:

Explanation:

Exercise 2: Finding the Better Word

Each of the following phrases uses the word "very" to indicate a stronger degree of the adjective.

- *Using a thesaurus and/or dictionary, find two new, concise adjectives to replace each phrase.*

- *Use each of the concise adjectives in a sentence.*

- *After the sentence, write a brief explanation of why you chose that synonym for that sentence.*

For example:

VERY COLD: frigid   freezing

Sentence 1: Planets beyond Mars have frigid climates because they are so far away from the sun.

Explanation: Frigid is defined simply as "intensely cold."

Sentence 2: Marcus was afraid that his freezing toes would develop frostbite.

Explanation: The definition of freezing has to do with "turning to ice."

1. **VERY PRETTY:** _____   _____
   Sentence 1:

   Explanation:

   Sentence 2:

   Explanation:

2. **VERY FRIENDLY:** _____   _____
   Sentence 1:

   Explanation:

   Sentence 2:

   Explanation:

3. **VERY FULL:** _____   _____
Sentence 1:

Explanation:

Sentence 2:

Explanation:

4. **VERY HAPPY:** _____   _____
Sentence 1:

Explanation:

Sentence 2:

Explanation:

5. **VERY DIRTY:** _____   _____
Sentence 1:

Explanation:

Sentence 2:

Explanation:

Using Vivid, Specific, Concrete Words

Consider these words: stuff, things, nice, mean. These words have so many meanings and shades of meaning that they are practically meaningless.

Consider this:

When you're told to "get your stuff," the "stuff" you're going to get depends totally on the context. If you're packing for vacation, "get your stuff" probably means to gather together your clothing, sports equipment, MP3 player, headphones, and whatever else you are planning to take with you on your trip. But, if you're in your last period class and your best friend has told you to "get your stuff," then he or she probably wants you to pick up your books, pens, and so on, and get ready to go home.

The word "thing" also requires more information to be understood. "Thing" is so vague that the person to whom you're speaking already needs to know what you are talking about in order to understand what you mean. For example, if you say, "Give me that thing," the other person needs to know what "thing" to give you.

And *nice*—is the cafeteria worker who gives you extra gravy on your mashed potatoes "nice"? Was Mother Teresa "nice"? If you think last night's dinner was "nice," and you describe your friend as "nice," does that mean you are planning to cook up your friend for tonight's meal?

Was Adolph Hitler "mean"? A specific adjective would be much more appropriate here.

The problem with words like "stuff," "things," "nice," and "mean" is that they are too vague or general in meaning.

Now consider *these* words: justice, love, patriotism, integrity.

These are all values, virtues. You will find it very difficult to find a person who will claim not to possess—or at least value—these traits, but you will find it equally difficult to find two or more people who will agree on what the words *mean*.

In just about all criminal court cases, the prosecution and defense represent absolutely opposite viewpoints. *Both*, however, will claim to seek justice. Mothers love their fathers; fathers love their daughters; the daughters love their boyfriends; and the boyfriends love their dogs, yet they do not all feel the *same emotion* for the objects of their affection. You may love pizza, but you probably will not marry one. More seriously, both Democrats and Republicans question their opponents' patriotism, but that does not indicate that members of either party are traitors. Even more perplexing is the question of integrity: does the person of integrity reveal his or her best friend's lie or keep quiet?

These *abstract terms* present the writer with essentially the same problem as vague, general words. They are open to interpretation, too broad in their range of meaning to communicate clearly with a reader.

By and large, the more abstract or general your writing is, the more unclear and boring it will be. The more concrete and specific your language is, the clearer and more vivid it will be.

Exercise 3: Using Appropriate Word Choice

In the following passages, underline the words and phrases that do not contribute anything specific to the your understanding or appreciation of the topic. Then, rewrite each passage using more vivid and specific words that communicate your message clearly.

Passage 1:

Josh Tollifson's first novel, *Another Saturday Night at the Wabash Laundry-Mat,* is an excellent book—funny, witty, with cleverly-drawn characters and a compelling plot. The plot is exciting and suspenseful, but there are times when the situations the characters find themselves in are just laughable. The characters themselves are all likeable, even when they say or do something maddening. They are just like real people. Finally, Tollifson's writing style is great. The language just flows. All in all, *Another Saturday Night at the Wabash Laundry-Mat* is a great read.

Revision:

Passage 2:

Dear Ms. Barkingwoolf:

A while ago, I was a guest at your hotel, and I feel I simply must let you know how I feel about my visit. First of all, the room was not at all what I expected. Neither the furniture nor the extra features were what the advertisement led me to believe they would be. I was also surprised by the quality of service I received from your staff. All in all, my stay in your hotel was not at all what I had thought it was going to be. I thought you'd want to know that.

Revision:

Passage 3:

It's actually very easy to get there from here. First of all, as you approach the corner, turn left. After a while, you'll see some trees and that's where you want to turn left again. When you pass a really neat-looking building, you'll go straight for a little bit, and then you'll turn right. (Don't go too far.) You'll notice how the road changes and everything looks different here. Follow the signs, and in a few minutes you'll want to turn left, then right, and then you're there.

Revision:

Abstract and Concrete Terms

Abstract terms refer to ideas or concepts; they are intangible—they are not physical and cannot be seen or touched.

Examples of abstract terms include *love, success, freedom, good, moral, democracy,* and any *-ism (chauvinism, Communism, feminism, racism, sexism)*. We are familiar with all of these concepts, and because we recognize them, we may *think* that we understand what they mean—but there will always be those who understand them differently.

This does not mean that we do not use abstract terms when we need them. We *need* to talk about ideas and concepts, and we need words that name them. But we must understand how imprecise their meanings are, how easily they can be interpreted differently, and ultimately how little the terms themselves communicate our exact ideas to someone else. Abstract terms are useful when we want to name ideas—as we do in thesis statements and topic sentences—but they're not enough to support the point you're trying to make without a good deal of definition, explanation, and development.

Concrete terms refer to objects or events that can actually be perceived by the senses. Examples of concrete terms include *spoon, table, juicy apple, black eye, sinus headache, red, hot, walking*. Because these terms refer to objects or activities we can see, hear, taste, touch, or smell, their ranges of meaning are pretty narrow. If you ask me what I mean by the word *spoon*, I can pick up a spoon and show it to you.

While abstract terms like *love* change meaning depending on their context, concrete terms like *dog* stay essentially the same. The words *moon, mist,* and *book* represent essentially the same objects in New York as they do in Los Angeles and Miami. Senior citizens in Maine and pre-schoolers in Texas will all recognize the same creature as a cat.

Politicians and advertisers generally prefer abstract terms to concrete terms. "Barbara Johnson is a woman of *integrity*, whose strong sense of *justice* and *equality* will allow her to represent *all* of her constituents with *fairness* and *compassion*" sounds good, but what does it mean? Does her "strong sense of justice" mean convicted criminals should be executed, or released on work-release programs? Does "equality" mean that everyone gets the same *benefit* or the same *opportunity*?

One way to clarify your use of vague abstractions is to find synonyms that imply *degrees* or *levels* of meaning. For example, while *love* is a broad term for a wide range of emotions, *affection, fondness,* and *warm regard* are clearer because they establish a milder form of love. *Ardor, passion,* and *adoration,* on the other hand, imply a strong, fiercer love. Choosing the best, clearest abstract term for your meaning is one of the most valid uses of the thesaurus—as long as you are careful to know exactly what the synonym you choose means and how to use it correctly.

An important element of making your essay painless to read, then, is choosing words that will communicate clearly and precisely so that you don't leave your reader with doubt regarding how to interpret what you've said.

Exercise 4: Using Concrete and Abstract Terms Effectively

Read the following list of abstract terms. For each word, list as many synonyms as you can find or think of. List them in order of magnitude from least to most intense.

For example:

Love: admiration, regard, tenderness, fondness, affection, love, devotion, ardor, passion

1. success:

2. freedom:

3. good:

4. moral:

5. liberal:

6. conservative:

7. betrayal:

8. honesty:

9. curiosity:

10. intelligence:

NOTE: Sometimes the abstract expression is really meaningless jargon. Again, novice writers tend to favor these expressions because they believe the abstract somehow sounds "better" or "smarter" than the concrete. Still, the fact remains that the abstract frequently means nothing, and the writing would be significantly improved by replacing it with a meaningful concrete term or expression.

Exercise 5: Using Concrete and Abstract Terms Effectively

Read the following list of meaningless abstract expressions. For each, state a concrete term that could be used in place of the abstract.

For example:

Assessment system: test

1. **communications device**

2. **information retrieval personnel**

3. **physical challenge**

4. **festive gathering**

5. **astute assembly**

General and Specific Terms

General terms and specific terms are not opposites, the way abstract and concrete terms are. Instead, they are opposite ends of a range of meanings. **General terms** refer to groups or categories, while **specific terms** refer to individuals. Both, however, are concrete in that they refer to objects or activities that can be perceived.

For example, *clothing* is a general term. It includes many different items. If your teacher were to write the word "clothing" on the blackboard, every student in the room would be able to form an image, but it is doubtful any two students would have formed the same—or even very similar—images. Even narrowing the range to "summer clothing" doesn't clarify the desired image that much.

We can make the group smaller with the less general term, *shorts*. Now everyone is at least picturing the same object, but the specifics of each image are still likely to vary widely.

Narrow the image further to *running shorts*. Now the image is clearer, and it's easier to begin to connect emotional associations, otherwise known as connotations, with the object. The images we form are likely to be fairly similar, with similar associations (comfort, exercise), so this less general, or more specific, term communicates more clearly than the more general, or less specific, terms before it.

We can become more and more specific. They can be *nylon running shorts, threadbare running shorts, threadbare nylon running shorts with frayed hems,* and so on. Eventually we do reach the point where the writer and the reader are picturing the same individual pair. With the necessary specific information, the reader is much more likely to appreciate whatever connotation, or emotional association, the writer wants to establish.

The more you rely on general terms, the more your writing will be vague, dull, and essentially unclear—certainly not a powerful essay. On the other hand, when you work to recreate the image, the experience, the idea for your reader in vivid, concrete terms, your writing will be more interesting, and your reader will "get it."

NOTE: Finding concrete specifics doesn't require a big vocabulary or a vivid imagination, just the willingness to recall what you already know. If you really can't find any examples or specifics to support your general conclusion, chances are your conclusion isn't valid, or you don't have enough information to write your essay.

You should gather as many concrete specifics in the prewriting stages of your essay as possible. If you have many concrete specifics at hand before you organize or draft, you're likely to think and write more easily and accurately. In fact, a sharp writer will use the number and quality of specifics he can recall as an important factor when deciding which topic to develop into a full essay and which potential topics to set aside.

Exercise 6: Using General and Specific Terms Effectively

In the following passages, underline the words and phrases that are too general to contribute anything meaningful to your understanding or appreciation of the topic. Then revise the passages, adding specific details so that they are clearer and more meaningful.

Passage 1:

It's my opinion that, if you're going to impose a dress code on students, then you should have one for teachers too. Teachers should dress like professionals. Their clothing should command respect. Their classrooms, too, should reflect their education and commitment to their profession. If students are to be expected to behave properly, then teachers should be expected to model appropriate behavior.

Revision:

Passage 2:

Holidays are fun. People decorate their homes and offices—sometimes even their cars. It's always prettier around a holiday, and it even smells better because people usually cook special food. Sometimes they exchange presents, dress up in fancy clothes, and play games or sing songs. I love holidays.

Revision:

Passage 3:

Last week's field trip to the museum was great. We saw so many interesting exhibits and learned all sorts of things about plants and animals, and the systems that help them maintain life. The tour guide was great. He explained everything and answered all of our questions—even the dumb ones. I hope we get to go on more field trips like this one this year.

Revision:

Writing Opportunity: *The Homework Essay: The Chapter, Book, or Article Summary*

A POPULAR ASSIGNMENT in many non-English classes is to require students to read current articles about the subject matter of the class. To prove that the student has actually completed the reading, and to demonstrate what the student has learned, the teacher requires the student to submit a summary of the article. Often, the teacher will assign the student to read a chapter in the textbook and write a summary. Writing chapter summaries is a very effective learning and study tool for students even if the summary is not a formal assignment,

While *all* of the traits of powerful essays are important in a summary, powerful word choice is crucial. Because the purpose of a summary is to communicate an understanding of the book, chapter, or article in your own words as concisely and clearly as possible, every word must carry as much weight as it can, thereby making powerful word choice extremely important.

In this writing opportunity, avoid vague, meaningless terms and be sure your abstract words are specific and clear.

Step 1: *Choose your topic*
What book, story, or article will you summarize? Make certain you know the book's full title, the author's full and correct name, and the genre (literary type).

Step 2: *Draft your main ideas*
Like the précis, your summary focuses on retelling information, but there is more room for interpretation and evaluation, so you will want to draft a thesis statement and statements introducing your major sub-points. These will, of course, focus on what you consider the most important points of the text you are summarizing.

Example:

> The January 16, 2006, *Top World News* article "Can We Achieve an Oil-less Society?" explores the benefits of a gasoline-price crisis and looks optimistically to a cleaner and energy-independent future.

> Reporter Candace Gonzalez insightfully examines three aspects of the evolution of the United States' energy policy. First, she demonstrates the unlikelihood that crude oil prices—and, therefore, gasoline prices—will ever return to pre-2005 levels. Secondly, she cites the increase in demand for cheaper alternative fuels. Finally, she follows this popular demand to its inevitable consequence—a marketplace that thrives on the competition to deliver reliable, cheap, and abundant energy.

Note that, while obviously the focus of the essay is not going to be on interpretation or evaluation, to say that the reporter "insightfully examines ..." is an evaluative statement. Also, to say that she "demonstrates" rather than "claims" and to assert that marketplace competition is the "inevitable consequence" are interpretations of the information in the article.

Notice also how careful selection of words like "insightful," "demonstrates," and "inevitable" allow the writer of the summary to place his or her own spin on the topic—impose his or her evaluation and interpretation—without adding length to what is supposed to be brief.

Remember, since you will not be able to repeat *every* detail from the original in the space allowed (usually a few paragraphs, 500–1,000 words or so, depending on the length of the original), this list of thesis and sub-point statements allows you to narrow your focus to those aspects that are most important.

Time Clue: Assume you have a week to read the article and write your summary. While you read, look for important points and think about how you will put them in your own words. As you encounter a new main idea in your reading, add it to your list. Then, when you're finished reading, all you need to do is draft the sentences in your own words.

Step 3: *Jot down the key supporting details of development*
If you have drafted a thesis statement as above (or a few different versions to see which one works best for you), this should help you to form your outline. While your précis followed the same order as the article you abstracted, your summary does not need to. Your summary will follow an order determined by you and established in your introduction.

Reread or skim the book, story, or article you are summarizing and write down the details that are most important to supporting what you have already said are the main ideas.

Remember to write everything *in your own words.*

Time Clue: Depending on the length of the original, once you have finished reading, you should not need more than an hour or two (for a story or article) or a day or two (for a full-length book) for this step.

Step 4: *Write your first draft*
Make it as complete as you can. As always, this is more than a freewrite because you have already identified the main ideas and listed the most important details.

This should take only as much time as it physically takes your hands to write or keyboard it.

Time Clue: Less than one day.

Step 5: *Revise and rewrite*

Set your draft aside for at least a day. Then read it over and look for holes in the information, any places where you could be clearer or more complete. Have you identified the *most important* points of the original? Are you providing enough of the *most important* details from the original to offer your reader a reasonable sample? Does your word choice reflect a strong understanding of the article or chapter? Have you chosen words that are strong, specific, and meaningful? You also want to pay attention to grammar, mechanics, spelling, and so on.

Use the scoring rubrics on pages 12, 35, 54, 78, and 114 and make certain your essay demonstrates your mastery.

Show your draft to one or two other people and have them read it and rate it according to the rubrics.

Rewrite the draft, fixing any of the problems you found when you reread it, and those that others found when you asked them to read it

Time Clue: You have just one day left for this step, but if you've been thinking, planning, and drafting carefully all along, this is plenty of time.

Step 6: *Turn in your summary*

Trait Six

Voice

TRAIT SIX:
VOICE

THE TERMS TONE AND VOICE share essentially the same meaning with very subtle differences. For all intents and purposes, they will be used synonymously in this book. Tone and Voice are what you strive to include in your writing and what your reader will hear in his or her head while reading your essay. It is a reflection of many factors: the topic, the audience, the reason for writing (or exigence), the rhetorical purpose of the writing, and—most importantly—*your attitude toward your topic and your audience.*

It's important to know *why* you're writing—both in terms of what is motivating you to write and what response you expect your audience to have after reading what you've written.

Exigence is the official term for the situation, the circumstances, that motivate you to write. There will be times when the exigence will be "because the teacher assigned it," but—as with purpose—if you can assume a rhetorical exigence, your writing will be much stronger.

Examples of Rhetorical Exigence (reasons for writing) include:

- the college to which you are applying requires a "personal statement;"

- you need to write a letter to a college (or potential employer) for information;

- you've been badly served (or well served) by a store and want to write a letter of complaint (or gratitude);

- you really enjoyed (or disliked) a book and want to write a review for *Amazon.com* or *BarnesandNoble.com,* and so forth.

In short, the exigence is whatever is motivating you to write. Even if you're writing for a school assignment or a test, you will write much better—and get better grades—if you write for a larger, firmer purpose.

Most rhetorical theories suggest four purposes for writing:
- to inform or explain
- to persuade
- to express what the writer thinks or believes
- to entertain.

Clearly, your purpose and audience will have tremendous impact on the tone or voice you use. For example, a letter to persuade a senator or member of Congress to support a particular bill should have a very different voice from a letter you're writing to your eight-year-old cousin to cheer him or her up.

Your exigence, too, will help determine your voice. It might be appropriate to sprinkle a negative review of a book with the occasional sarcastic tone, but it would not be in your best interest to be sarcastic to a potential employer or college admissions officer.

Tone and Voice are usually discussed in terms similar to the following:

informal, conversational	formal, respectful, academic
light, humorous, comic	serious
personal, subjective	impersonal, objective
casual, offhanded	fervent, passionate
plain, simple	ornate, elaborate

A knowledge of your audience and your purpose for writing is essential when deciding the appropriate tone and voice to assume in your writing.

Make Yours Better!

Note that the informal, conversational voice of this essay seems completely inappropriate for an academic subject.

The Amber Room is missing. The Amber Room wasn't an actual room, but it was a collection of panels decorated with amber, mirrors, and jewels. The panels could be attached to the walls of a room, creating an amber room.

In 1716, the King of Prussia gave the room to Russian Czar Peter the Great. After Peter died, his widow, Catherine moved the panels from the winter palace in St. Petersburg to her summer home in Tsarskoye Selo. She also had the panels embellished. When Hitler invaded the Soviet Union in 1941, he stole the room and is said to have had it transported to Königsburg, a city in Germany. The room has been missing since the end of World War II when the allies bombed Königsburg.

Now no one knows where the room is or what happened to it. There are several theories. Most historians assume the room was destroyed. Some suggest that the room was sunk in a boat in the Baltic Sea, or it was hidden in an abandoned mine in Thuringia.

The fate of this Amber Room will probably never be known. It was very beautiful and would be worth about $142 million dollars today.

- Repetitive word choice and the absence of vivid descriptors make this opening paragraph flat and dull.

- Again, sentence structure is correct, and there is some variety, but there is nothing enticing in the presentation of this information. Supporting details are sufficient and accurate, but not compelling.

- The concluding sentence lacks the necessary transition to complete the nostalgic tone that should be present.

Essay Critique

In terms of five of the six essential traits, there is nothing wrong with this essay; it is perfectly adequate. The author does not, however, make any attempt to adopt a voice of authority, or even a strictly formal or informal voice.

This essay receives a score of ① on the:

Voice Rubric

5 = The essay shows strong evidence of an attempt to create a narrative voice, but the effect is not yet fully achieved, or reflects the writer's only voice—regardless of topic, purpose, or audience.

4 = DEVELOPING
A narrative voice is suggested, but inconsistently controlled, and may not be appropriate to the topic, purpose, and audience

3 = The essay shows uneven evidence of experimentation with word choice and sentence structure to achieve a desired effect. The reader is probably able to infer a narrative voice.

2 = The essay shows little evidence of experimentation with word choice and sentence structure to achieve a desired effect.

①= NOVICE
Narrative voice is flat and dull, limited by knowledge of vocabulary and sentence structure. Language is vague, unintentionally unclear or ambiguous, and shows a lack of control.

Examining Samples of a Variety of Narrative Voices (formal, informal)

Read the following two versions of the same article. One is written in a formal, academic voice. The other is more informal, conversational. Either voice is "correct," depending on the audience and purpose of the article. You would not submit to a teacher or professor an essay that is too conversational. Nor would you submit an overly formal article to a publication that strives to maintain a friendlier tone with its readers.

The key is not to learn the "right" voice for your writing, but to experiment with a number of different voices and learn to use the appropriate voice for the appropriate topic, purpose, and audience.

The Orphan Trains[1]

Through the second half of the nineteenth century and the first quarter of the twentieth, a daring and innovative approach to childhood poverty and delinquency was devised and enacted. Eastern cities, especially New York, were flooded with immigrants who quickly found that the rumors they'd heard in Europe of streets lined with gold and vast money-making opportunities at every corner were largely exaggerated. The poor, uneducated, and unemployed collected in swelling slums with two or three families sharing the same two-room tenement. Hopelessness led to vice. Vice led to neglect; and soon New York's streets were swarming with hungry, neglected children. One young minister came up with an idea to ameliorate the situation. Send the children West.

The story of the "Orphan Train" endeavor to rescue these poor and homeless children begins in the 1850s, when thousands of children roamed the streets of New York in search of money, food, and shelter. Many sold matches, rags, or newspapers to survive. For protection against street violence, they banded together and formed gangs. Police, faced with the growing problem, finally resorted to arresting vagrant children—some as young as five—and locking them up with adult criminals.

In 1853, Charles Loring Brace, a young minister, became obsessed with the plight of these children. A member of a prominent Connecticut family, Brace had come to New York to complete his seminary training. Horrified by the conditions he saw on the street, Brace was persuaded there was only one way to help these "children of unhappy fortune."

"The great duty," he wrote, "is to get them utterly out of their surroundings and to send them away to kind Christian homes in the country."

In 1853, Brace founded the Children's Aide Society to arrange the trips, raise the money, and obtain the legal permissions needed for relocation. Between 1854 and 1929, more than 100,000 children were sent, via orphan trains, to new homes in rural America. Recognizing the need for labor in the expanding farm country, Brace believed that American farmers would welcome homeless children, take them into their homes, and treat them as their own.

Placement into new families was informal. Handbills heralded the distribution of cargos of needy children. As the trains pulled into towns, the youngsters were cleaned up and displayed on makeshift stages before crowds of prospective parents.

The Children's Aid Society liked to point with pride to success stories, like those of street boys Andrew Burke and John Brady who grew up to become governors of North Dakota and of Alaska, respectively. But the record of placements was mixed. Some of the farmers saw the children as nothing more than a source of cheap labor. There was evidence of abuse by some foster parents. Many of the older boys simply ran away; some children were rejected by their new parents.

But even those for whom the journey ultimately was a triumph found the transition from one life to another painful and confusing. "I would give a hundred worlds like this," wrote one child from her new comfortable home, "if I could see my mother."

Brace himself grappled with the dilemma: "When a child of the streets stands before you in rags, with a tear-stained face, you cannot easily forget him. And yet, you are perplexed what to do. The human soul is difficult to interfere with. You hesitate how far you should go."

The Orphan Trains[2]

The "Orphan Trains" were a new way to deal with poverty and crime among children and teenagers in the late 1800's and early 1900's. People who'd left their native countries in Europe to come to America came to cities in the East, especially New York City. These people soon found out that what they'd heard in Europe—that America's streets were paved with gold, and there was a way to make a million on every block—just wasn't true. These poor, illiterate, and jobless folk found their way to the slums that were growing more and more crowded. They had no hope. They began to drink. Some turned to petty crimes to get the money to drink. They neglected their children, and these children hit the street, too, becoming beggars and criminals alongside their parents.

It all began in the 1850's. There were thousands of kids just roaming the streets looking for money, food, and a place to sleep. They sold junk like rags and matches to make money. They formed gangs to protect themselves from being beaten up by other kids in other gangs. In no time at all, the problem had gotten so close to out of control that police really had no choice but to lock up the kids. Some of these children were as young as five, and they were locked up with adult criminals.

Clearly, this was not a good thing.

So in 1853, a young minister whose name was Charles Loring Brace became concerned about these kids and their problem. Brace was a member of a rich and powerful family in Connecticut, and he was in New York to finish his seminary training so that he could be a minister. He was horrified by what he saw on the streets and figured there was only one way to help these kids he called, "children of unhappy fortune."

His idea was simply to help the kids by getting them out of town.

Then he founded the Children's Aid Society and used this group to get the money and the permission to transport the kids. He also made the travel plans through this group. The trains carrying these kids were called "Orphan Trains," and more than 100,000 kids were taken from the cities to new homes in the country. The farms in the Midwest were expanding and needed labor (this was before modern farm machinery was invented), so Brace figured that farmers would be glad to have these homeless city kids come live with them. He figured the farmers would take them right into their homes and adopt them as if they were their own kids.

There was neither rhyme nor reason to how kids were matched up with parents and placed in new homes. Fliers were given out and posted that said a train would be arriving full of kids, and anyone who wanted one should come to the train station. The kids were given a "cat's lick and a promise" clean-up and sent out to stand on the station platform like puppies on display at the pound, posing for their hoped-for parents, silently mugging, "Choose me, choose me."

There were some awesome successes. Andrew Burke and John Brady both grew up to be state governors—Burke in North Dakota, and Brady in Alaska. But there were a lot of failures, too. A lot of the farmers thought of the kids as nothing more than cheap labor. Some parents abused their kids. A lot of the older boys simply ran away, and some kids were kicked out by their new parents.

Even the kids who made it had it tough. One girl was taken in by nice people and given pretty clothes to wear and good food to eat, but she wrote, "I would give a hundred worlds like this if I could see my mother."

Brace had no idea really what the right thing to do was. He wrote, "When a child of the streets stands before you in rags, with a tear-stained face, you cannot easily forget him. And yet, you are perplexed what to do. The human soul is difficult to interfere with. You hesitate how far you should go."

Factors That Help to Determine Voice

After you've read the two preceding passages, decide which has the more formal or academic voice and which has the more informal or conversational voice. Then, list those items that you think contribute to that particular voice.

What you'll find is that there is no one language feature that controls voice and tone. Everything—word choice, sentence structure, attention to conventions, even organizational patterns and the Development and Elaboration—has an impact on tone and voice. That is one reason why it is important for you to begin to master all of the other traits before you begin to worry about voice and tone.

The Role of Word Choice in Voice and Tone

- **Slang, colloquial, and "informal" words** will give your writing an informal, conversational tone, but you must be careful to choose the most appropriate language for your intended audience. You would not, for example, fill a letter of application to a Midwestern college with New England colloquialisms. Nor would you close a letter to a potential employer you knew to be middle–aged and culturally conservative with the slang expression, "Peace Out."

- **Clinical or professional terms,** when used correctly, will give your writing a formal, academic tone and help you achieve an authoritative voice.

- **Jargon,** on the other hand, is professional language pushed to such an extreme that it becomes almost like slang—understood and appreciated by a relative few. The fields of medicine, law, and computer technology have developed specific jargons that both streamline communication with individuals inside the discipline and identify and exclude "outsiders."

   Basically, it's an issue of audience. If you are an "insider" writing to other "insiders," then it might be appropriate to use jargon and slang. If, however, you are an "outsider," or you are writing to "outsiders," then to use the "insider" language will serve only to alienate you from a major portion of your intended audience.

NOTE: The real secret to creating and maintaining a powerful voice in a piece of writing is to make certain that the voice—formal, conversational, angry, apologetic—is *your voice.* If you are not a New Englander, it would not be realistic for you to use New England colloquialisms unless they are, somehow a normal part of your speech. Moreover, it would actually be almost laughable for you to try to appear "cool" by using contemporary slang if, again, such words and expressions are not a part of your normal speech.

The Role of Sentence Structure and Variety in Voice and Tone

- **Simple sentences** generally tend to lend a simplistic, child-like, and informal tone to writing.

- **Varied structures**, especially the judicial use of compound and complex sentences, will give your writing a more formal and academic tone. Placing subordinate clauses before the main clause makes the tone more formal and academic, but you do need to be careful not to overuse this sentence formation.

- **Sentence fragments**—if used carefully—can help to create an informal, conversational tone, *but they should never be used in formal, academic writing.*

- **Interrogative and exclamatory sentences** tend to make a passage sound conversational. *In formal, academic writing, you should absolutely avoid using a question as a thesis sentence, topic sentence, or transition.*

The Role of Grammar and Mechanics in Voice and Tone

- **Verb tense:** Usually the subject matter itself will determine the appropriate verb tense, but a narrative in the present tense tends to be more informal and conversational than a narrative in the past tense.

- **Dashes and commas:** While dashes may be used in some of the same situations as commas and semi-colons, dashes tend to create a conversational tone; whereas, commas and semi-colons lend an academic tone.

- **Contractions** create an informal, conversational tone. Many teachers and professors, as well as some word processing grammar-check applications, consider contractions to be bad usage.

The Role of Narrative Point of View in Voice and Tone

It is important for you to understand the impact of narrative point of view in your own writing.

- **First person point of view** is, of course, appropriate for *all* writing in which you refer to or talk about yourself: autobiographical essays, application essays or letters, etc. As soon as you use a first person pronoun, however, you have established an essentially conversational tone.

  First person point of view is *not* appropriate in any formal, academic writing in which you are not the subject.

- **Direct address** is, by its very nature, conversational. Even in an autobiographical piece, you may not need or want to speak directly to your reader.

  Like first person, use of the second person (you) is *not* appropriate in any formal, academic settings.

- **Third person point of view** is your absolute best option for all of the essays, reports, research papers, and other presentations you will write in school and in your career. If your goal is to maintain a formal or academic tone, use the third person.

Exercise 1: Changing the Tone

Revise the following passages, giving them a more formal or academic tone. In order to do so, you will be rewriting the passages, making major, as opposed to superficial, changes.

Passage 1:

Do you believe in time travel? ESP? UFOs? Well, there are lots of people who do, and they'll tell you that as far back as World War II the government began experimenting with time travel—with disastrous results.

It was called either "The Philadelphia Project" or "The Phoenix Project," depending on the sources you read. But what happened was that the Navy was trying to find a way to make a ship invisible to the enemy's radar. The test ship was the USS Eldridge that was stationed at the Philadelphia Navy Yard. They actually succeeded in making the ship "invisible" to radar, but that wasn't all. The ship actually disappeared! Became invisible!

When the ship reappeared, the sailors on board were a mess. They were confused. disoriented. Some had somehow become "melted" into the ship's structure—as if they'd been transported to another dimension and then unsuccessfully transported back. All of the survivors were labeled "crazy." They were discharged, and the whole thing was hushed up.

Revision:

Passage 2:

Project Blue Book was a look into UFOs. It was conducted by the United States Air Force and lasted 21 years. Starting in 1948, Blue Book looked at some 12,600 supposed UFO sightings. Blue Book couldn't explain 701 of the reports it had investigated. But it never came right out and said that there were really aliens flying our friendly skies either. As you'd expect, the U.S. government straddled the fence and wouldn't commit either way—either there are aliens or there aren't. They decided that these 701 mysterious sightings didn't threaten national security, Project Blue Book was shut down in 1969.

The guy who'd been the boss of Blue Book, Dr. Edward U. Condon, said that there was no chance that any intelligent life elsewhere—what he called ILE— would come to us within the next 10,000 years. The thing is, just because they maybe haven't been here yet, how could he know when they will or won't be coming?

After they shut down Blue Book, all of its files were opened to the public. But other documents not held by Project Blue Book are still top secret. Private UFO groups have sued to have those files also opened to the public.

Dr. J. Allen Hynek, who'd worked on Blue Book, continued the investigation. His agency—the Center for UFO Studies (CUFOS)—cranked into gear in 1973. Some 80 percent of the thousands of UFO reports investigated by CUFOS can be explained. Still, that 20 percent is still a mystery.

Revision:

Passage 3:

So the Jersey Devil is supposed to be this mythical creature that lives in the Pine Barrens of southern New Jersey. It was supposedly born some time in the middle of the 1700's to a Mrs. Leeds. It was her thirteenth child—an unlucky number to begin with—and when the baby was being born, Mrs. Leeds supposedly yelled at the top of her lungs, "I'm tired of children, I hope it's a devil!"

Well, as the saying goes, you have to be careful what you wish for, because Mrs. Leeds got her wish. Her thirteenth child was a weird creature with a horse's head, bat's wings, and a forked tail. After it was born, it flew away into the night. Some people claim that this Mrs. Leeds was a witch and this kid's father was the devil himself.

Since then, this "Jersey Devil," as Mrs. Leeds' thirteenth kid came to be known, has supposedly been seen by over 2,000 people including famous guys like Joseph Bonaparte, a former king of Spain and brother to the famous Napoleon. He claimed to have seen the Jersey Devil in 1816 or 1839 or something like that. Through the years, farmers have complained that some weird creature that makes a piercing scream and leaves weird tracks has killed their sheep and chickens. Some people even claimed that the Jersey Devil carried away their babies!

Sightings of this crazy creature have decreased in recent decades—probably because people don't want to be called crazy so they don't report seeing him. I guess we'll never really know whether the Jersey Devil really exists, or what he really is, but it's fun to imagine.

Revision:

Exercise 2: Changing the Tone

Revise the following passages, giving them a more informal or conversational tone. In order to do so, you will be rewriting the passages, making major, as opposed to superficial, changes.

Passage 1: From Abraham Lincoln's Second Inaugural Address

At this second appearing to take the oath of the Presidential office there is less occasion for an extended address than there was at the first. Then a statement somewhat in detail of a course to be pursued seemed fitting and proper. Now, at the expiration of four years, during which public declarations have been constantly called forth on every point and phase of the great contest which still absorbs the attention and engrosses the energies of the nation, little that is new could be presented. The progress of our arms, upon which all else chiefly depends, is as well known to the public as to myself, and it is, I trust, reasonably satisfactory and encouraging to all. With high hope for the future, no prediction in regard to it is ventured.

On the occasion corresponding to this four years ago all thoughts were anxiously directed to an impending civil war. All dreaded it, all sought to avert it. While the inaugural address was being delivered from this place, devoted altogether to *saving* the Union without war, urgent agents were in the city seeking to *destroy* it without war—seeking to dissolve the Union and divide effects by negotiation. Both parties deprecated war, but one of them would *make* war rather than let the nation survive, and the other would *accept* war rather than let it perish, and the war came.

Revision:

Passage 2: From "A Letter from Christopher Columbus to the King & Queen of Spain"

Most High and Mighty Sovereigns,

In obedience to your Highnesses' commands, and with submission to superior judgment, I will say whatever occurs to me in reference to the colonization and commerce of the Island of Espanola, and of the other islands, both those already discovered and those that may be discovered hereafter.

In the first place, as regards the Island of Espanola: Inasmuch as the number of colonists who desire to go thither amounts to two thousand, owing to the land being safer and better for farming and trading, and because it will serve as a place to which they can return and from which they can carry on trade with the neighboring islands:

1. That in the said island there shall be founded three or four towns, situated in the most convenient places, and that the settlers who are there be assigned to the aforesaid places and towns.

2. That for the better and more speedy colonization of the said island, no one shall have liberty to collect gold in it except those who have taken out colonists' papers, and have built houses for their abode, in the town in which they are, that they may live united and in greater safety.

        •••

4. That there shall he a church, and parish priests or friars to administer the sacraments, to perform divine worship, and for the conversion of the Indians.

        •••

8. That one per centum of all the gold that may be found shall be set aside for building churches and adorning the same, and for the support of the priests or friars belonging to them; and, if it should be thought proper to pay any thing to the alcaldes or notaries for their services, or for ensuring the faithful perforce of their duties, that this amount shall be sent to the governor or treasurer who may be appointed there by your Highnesses.

9. As regards the division of the gold, and the share that ought to be reserved for your Highnesses, this, in my opinion, must be left to the aforesaid governor and treasurer, because it will have to be greater or less according to the quantity of gold that may be found. Or, should it seem preferable, your Highnesses might, for the space of one year, take one half, and the collector the other, and a better arrangement for the division be made afterward.

        •••

Revision:

Passage 3: From Abraham Lincoln's Gettysburg Address on November 19, 1863

Fourscore and seven years ago our fathers brought forth on this continent a new nation, conceived in liberty and dedicated to the proposition that all men are created equal.

Now we are engaged in a great civil war, testing whether that nation or any nation so conceived and so dedicated can long endure. We are met on a great battlefield of that war. We have come to dedicate a portion of it as a final resting place for those who died here that the nation might live. This we may, in all propriety do. But in a larger sense, we cannot dedicate, we cannot consecrate, we cannot hallow this ground. The brave men, living and dead who struggled here have hallowed it far above our poor power to add or detract. The world will little note nor long remember what we say here, but it can never forget what they did here.

It is rather for us the living, we here be dedicated to the great task remaining before us—that from these honored dead we take increased devotion to that cause for which they here gave the last full measure of devotion—that we here highly resolve that these dead shall not have died in vain, that this nation shall have a new birth of freedom, and that government of the people, by the people, for the people shall not perish from the earth.

Revision:

Writing Opportunity: *The Letter of Interest*

THROUGHOUT YOUR LIFE there will be times when the most effective way for you to communicate with another person is by writing a letter. Even if that letter exists only in the virtual world of a computer hard drive and is transmitted electronically to its recipient, the rules of powerful writing apply if you want your reader to understand your point, and if you want your letter to accomplish its purpose.

The letter of introduction or interest is usually your chance to make a first impression. Unlike a phone call, the letter allows you to fully plan this first impression, revising it to near perfection. There will be no surprises for you when writing the letter. You will not have to "think on your feet" as you would if the communication were face-to-face.

In letter writing, voice and tone are especially important because the letter—more than any other form you might write—represents *you*. If you are angry or disappointed about a product or service, this will rightly impact the tone of your letter. If you are introducing yourself, or requesting information from a school you hope to attend, or contacting an employer for whom you hope to work, this will rightly impact the tone of your letter. While the content of the letter is indeed important, the tone and voice of the letter are equally important, as they give the reader the clearest sense of who the writer is.

Step 1: *Identify your audience and decide why you will write for this particular audience*

Think about individuals in your area whose jobs have to do with a career that interests you. Think about a school you might want to attend or a program in which you might want to participate.

Think about what you are going to ask this person or group. You might ask for as little as the opportunity to talk to him or her about how to begin and build a career in his or her field. You may want to ask about the possibility of working for him or her part time, or of serving as an intern. You may need to know the eligibility requirements and application process for the organization you hope to join.

Step 2: *Develop your purpose statement*

Always remember that good writing is the result of good thinking. If you can't explain in one sentence your purpose for writing, you probably don't understand it yourself. After all, it is in the development of this purpose statement that allows you to begin to show the reader of the letter who *you* are.

For example:

Let's say you're writing a letter of introduction to a woman in your town who operates a laboratory that produces dental fixtures—crowns, dentures, bridgework, etc. You are interested in the possibility of speaking to her or ask about the type of education and experience she needed to do this work, and you would like to ask if you might actually come and see her lab and watch her work.

Since you don't want to waste this woman's time (even the amount of time it might take her to read a brief letter), and you do want a positive response from her, you will want to state your request as clearly and succinctly as possible—and as near the beginning of your letter as possible.

> As a ninth grader at Scrapplepot Regional High School who is interested in the field of dental prosthetics, I was hoping to ask for a few minutes of your time to talk to you about your work and maybe even visit your laboratory.

Notice how the writer has been briefly introduced him—a ninth grader at Scrapplepot Regional High School—and stated the purpose of the letter—to ask for a few minutes to talk and perhaps a visit to the lab.

Now that the essential information is established, the recipient can take her time to read the rest of the letter and decide whether or not to grant the request.

Step 3: *Brainstorm and jot down your supporting details*

In this case, the supporting points of your letter include whatever details about yourself will help to establish your credibility as a person interested in the field of dental prosthetics, and your plans for the meeting with this professional so that she can know in advance that you do not intend to waste her time.

Now is the time to make a list of the supporting details for your letter.

Time Clue: Let's assume you've been given one week for this letter (the assignment was made on Monday and the letter is due Friday). You should complete your purpose statement and supporting details list on Monday.

Step 4: *Organize*

Think as your intended reader would. What is a logical order in which to discuss your ideas? Will it be more helpful to discuss you and your interest in her field, or will it be better first to establish the amount of time you want to spend with her and what you hope to do with that time?

Since you've got time and your letter will not be long (certainly no longer than one page), you might actually want to write several rough drafts, trying out different ways to present yourself and your request.

Time Clue: If you're going to have a good final draft to turn in Friday, you'll want to complete these first drafts on Tuesday.

Step 7: *Revise and rewrite*

Set your draft letters aside for the night.

On Thursday, read them as if you were the person to whom you are writing. Which of your drafts

- presents yourself most completely and accurately, and in the best possible light?

- presents yourself and your request in the clearest language? In the most logical order?

- has the appropriate tone and the voice that sounds most like you?

Use the scoring rubrics on pages 154 - 159 to help you select which of your drafts is most worth revising.

Show your drafts to one or two other people to be read and rated according to the rubrics.

Select the draft that will give you the best final letter and revise it, fixing any of the problems you found when you reread it, and those that others found when you asked them to read it.

Time Clue: All revision and rewriting is done Thursday.

Step 8: *Your letter is finished. Submit it.*

Appendix

Trait-by-Trait Scoring Guide for the Novice Level

DEVELOPMENT AND ELABORATION

5 = The main idea of the essay is clear, but the overall discussion is weakened by inconsistent development and elaboration. Some supporting points tend to be underdeveloped (too few details, examples, anecdotes, supporting facts, etc.). Some minor irrelevancies likewise weaken the essay.

4 = **DEVELOPING**
The main idea of the essay is suggested. There are supporting details with some elaboration, but supporting points are underdeveloped. Some of the points or development my be tangential or irrelevant to the topic, purpose, and audience.

3 = The main idea of the essay is suggested. There are supporting points without elaboration, or some of the elaboration is irrelevant to the topic, purpose, or audience.

2 = The main idea of the essay is suggested. There may be supporting points, but they are not elaborated upon. Some of the details may be irrelevant to the topic, purpose, or audience.

1 = **NOVICE**
The main idea of the essay is implicit but not clear. There tend to be too few or no supporting points and the details presented tend not to be elaborated upon. Some of the details or elaboration may be irrelevant to the topic, purpose, or audience

ORGANIZATION

5 = The organizational plan of the essay is clear and consistently applied but is obvious and/or formulaic (e.g., the five-paragraph essay), thus limiting the essay's overall effectiveness.

4 = **DEVELOPING**

An appropriate but obvious organizational plan is apparent and generally followed, but jumps or gaps distract the reader.

3 = An organizational plan is apparent but followed inconsistently so that the reader may be distracted by jumps or gaps. The apparent plan may not be the most appropriate for the topic, purpose, or audience.

2 = An organizational plan is suggested, but the overall effect of the essay seems more intuitive or accidental than intentional. Deviations from the plan are unintentional and distracting. The apparent plan may not be the most appropriate for the topic, purpose, or audience.

1 = **NOVICE**

The essay lacks an intentional organizational plan. Ideas are presented simply as they occurred to the writer.

SENTENCE STRUCTURE

5 = There is an attempt to vary sentence length and structure, but it appears to be variety for variety's sake rather than topic, purpose, audience, and voice determining appropriate sentence structure. Minor problems in structure, grammar, and/or word choice make them less effective than they might be. These errors can be corrected with minor revision (insertion of words, creation of appositives and/or subordinate clauses, etc.).

4 = **DEVELOPING**
There is evidence of experimentation with sentence variety, but this variety is forced and may result in awkward and inappropriate constructions.

3 = Basic sentence formation (simple sentence, compound sentence) is accurate. There is an attempt to experiment with more sophisticated structures (complex, compound-complex sentences). Problems in structure may create convoluted sentences that require substantial revision (number agreement, rearrangement of phrases and clauses to make a fragment a sentence, etc.) to correct.

2 = Sentences are complete and structured correctly, but there is little or no variety in sentence structure.

1 = **NOVICE**
There is little or no variety in sentence structure. Some sentence structure errors (fragments, run-ons) indicate a lack of control.

CONVENTIONS

5 = Essay is largely free of basic surface errors. Errors that do appear (semi-colon, complex subject-verb agreement, etc.) suggest an attempt to experiment with more sophisticated language and may interfere with the reader's understanding, requiring extensive revision.

4 = **DEVELOPING**
Essay is largely free of basic surface errors (spelling, elementary punctuation, capitalization, etc.), but correctness of language is largely governed by simplicity of language.

3 = Surface errors may be frequent but do not severely interfere with the reader's understanding of the essay. Correctness of language is largely governed by simplicity of language.

2 = Basic surface errors (spelling, elementary punctuation, capitalization, etc.) are frequent and varied enough to indicate a lack of understanding of the fundamentals of standard written English. Frequency and variety of errors interfere with the reader's understanding.

1 = **NOVICE**
Surface errors may be frequent and extreme, and severely interfere with the reader's understanding of the essay. Correctness of language is largely governed by simplicity of language.

WORD CHOICE

5 = Word choice shows strong attempts at vividness, but vague and inexact language predominates. Figurative language (similes, metaphors, allusions) is unoriginal, and does not really contribute to the overall effect of the essay.

4 = **DEVELOPING**
Attempts at vividness are more frequent and intentional, but miss the mark, often resulting in clichés, awkward constructions, and an overuse of adjective-noun and adverb-verb phrases, especially overuse of amplifiers like "very," "truly," etc.

3 = Infrequent and tentative attempts at vividness result in clichés and awkward constructions.

2 = Word choice is vague, simplistic, and repetitive. There is no real attempt to use figurative language for clearer, more effective communication.

1 = **NOVICE**
Word choice is inexact and vague, largely affected by the writer's limited vocabulary. There is no real attempt to use figurative language for clearer, more effective communication.

TONE AND VOICE

5 = The essay shows strong evidence of an attempt to create a narrative voice, but the effect is not yet fully achieved, or reflects the writer's only voice—regardless of topic, purpose, or audience.

4 = **DEVELOPING**

A narrative voice is suggested, but inconsistently controlled, and may not be appropriate to the topic, purpose, and audience.

3 = The essay shows uneven evidence of experimentation with word choice and sentence structure to achieve a desired effect. The reader is probably able to infer a narrative voice.

2 = The essay shows little evidence of experimentation with word choice and sentence structure to achieve a desired effect.

1 = **NOVICE**

Narrative voice is flat and dull, limited by knowledge of vocabulary and sentence structure. Language is vague, unintentionally unclear or ambiguous, and shows a lack of control.